SOPHOCLES

TRANSLATED BY

JOHN TIPTON

FOREWORD BY

STANLEY LOMBARDO

FLOOD EDITIONS

CHICAGO

Ajax

τέως δὲ κούφοις πνεύμασιν βόσκου, νέαν

ψυχὴν ἀτάλλων, μητρὶ τῇδε χαρμονήν.

CONTENTS

Aeschylus is famously reported to have said that Greek
tragedy consisted of leftovers from the great banquet of
Homer. Whatever he meant by "leftovers," Aeschylus'
dictum reminds us that the Athenian audience at the
original production of Sophocles' *Ajax* would have
Homer's portrayal of the hero clearly in mind and
that much of their interest as spectators would have
been to see how Sophocles played his hero off against
Homer's and positioned his drama with respect to
Homer's epic frame.

Ajax' career in Homer is framed by silence, his supe-
rior silence when Agamemnon praises his preparedness
to fight in *Iliad* 4, and his icy silence when Odysseus
tries to apologize in the Underworld (*Odyssey* 11) for
that business with Achilles' armor that is the backstory

of Sophocles' play. Nor does he have much to say in between. When Homer does have him speak he is very blunt. Here is one of the first things he says in the *Iliad* (Book 7), a short speech delivered as he stands before Hector like "a Greek wall" as the two prepare to duel, "the gristle that was his face arranged in a smile." Thrusting that face into Hector's, Ajax says:

> Take a good look, Hector. This is what
> The heroes are like in the Greek army
> Even when Achilles isn't here smashing skulls.
> He's back there with the ships now,
> Nursing his grudge against Agamemnon,
> But we still have a few good men to fight you.
> More than a few. It's your move.

The duel was called for darkness just as Ajax was about to overpower his Trojan opponent, and the two heroes exchanged gifts, Ajax receiving from Hector the sword upon which he impales himself in Sophocles' play.

It can't have helped Ajax' general mood that as great as he was he was not quite a winner, always second, and not only to the incomparable Achilles. In the funeral games for Patroclus, whose body Ajax had almost single-handedly rescued from the Trojans (he was later to do the same for Achilles' body), Ajax loses to Diomedes in armed combat, to the otherwise inconspicuous Polypoetes in the weight throw, and in the wrestling event to the wily Odysseus who would be awarded Achilles' divine armor after his death and who would figure so largely in Sophocles' drama.

For all his runner-up karma and disdain for fine words, Homer's Ajax is nevertheless a thoroughly noble figure, as sound of mind and character as of body. Increasing his appeal to the Athenian audience, Ajax was from Salamis, the island just a mile off shore from Piraeus, the port of Athens. Ajax boasts of his provenance before his duel with Hector: "I was born and bred in Salamis, and I know I am no fool." Sophocles could count on considerable shock value in opening his play with this hero slaughtering and torturing pigs in the deluded belief that he was exacting revenge from the Greek leaders who had cheated him of his prize. This unmitigated disgrace will be followed by another, the hero's suicide, at the play's mid-point, after which, as John Tipton points out in the afterword to his translation, a series of remarkable reversals takes place as the play turns itself inside out, Ajax' corpse dominating the stage.

But it is Sophocles' treatment of Ajax after he comes to his senses and realizes what he has done that is the heart of the play. In a series of speeches, and principally the speech known as the Renunciation Speech (lines 646–92), the Athenian playwright takes us into the mind of his hero in a way that Homer never did, showing us that in spite of his disgrace and shame, his heroism, which is his untrammeled will, is intact. Ajax thinks as he talks, and as he talks he comes not only to solutions to the problems that confront him—problems concerning his child, his wife, his parents, and his own shame—but also to a deep understanding of the fundamental problem of human life, time itself, which has brought the ancient honor by which Ajax lived into darkness. There is a complex passion and intelligence at work in these lines, among the best in Sophocles and all Greek literature, and it is a tribute to Tipton's skill as a translator that he is able to capture the tone and movement of this passage, of a great man talking aloud and determining his end. Here as everywhere in this translation there is the sense that Tipton, surely, in part, because of the unique formal constraints he has placed upon himself, has looked closely *into* rather than simply *at* Sophocles' Greek, has locked eyebrows with the old Aegean dramatist.

STANLEY LOMBARDO

University of Kansas

AJAX

CHARACTERS

ATHENA

ODYSSEUS

AJAX

CHORUS OF SAILORS

TECMESSA

MESSENGER

TEUCER

MENELAUS

AGAMEMNON

ATHENA

Often, Odysseus, I have seen you

on the hunt pressing an enemy.

Now you come to Ajax' tent

at the end of the line.

So the trail leads you here

with fresh tracks and you see

they go in and come out.

You bloodhound—snout to the ground!

Yes, the man just went in,

his head sweating, his hands bloody.

But no need to look inside—

he is there.

       Tell me, why

the hurry?

          Perhaps I can help.

The voice of Athena—my goddess!
I know you—can't see you
but that voice in my head
rings like a bright bronze horn.

You know me too well—yes,
I've been circling this soldier's tent.
The trail leads here, no further.
Last night something very strange happened.
It looks like Ajax is responsible.
No one saw clearly—only guesses—
and I want to confirm it.
We just discovered a bloody mess:
our captured cattle all dead, butchered
along with the herdsmen watching them.
Everyone suspects Ajax of it because
a picket said he saw him
running with a freshly bloodied weapon,
moving fast.
                    I came right away
and picked up the trail along
with other tracks I don't recognize.

As always you're just in time;
you can steer me from here.

ATHENA

Yes, Odysseus, I watched the progress
of your hunt with some interest.

ODYSSEUS

How have I done, my goddess?

ATHENA

He is the man you want.

ODYSSEUS

What stupidity drove him to it?

ATHENA

An uncontrollable anger over Achilles' arms.

ODYSSEUS

Then why kill animals and shepherds?

ATHENA

He thought you stained his hands.

ODYSSEUS

So he planned to attack *Greeks*?

ATHENA

And would have but for me.

ODYSSEUS

How could he be so bold?

ATHENA

He moved under cover of night.

ODYSSEUS

Then why didn't he reach us?

ATHENA

He was just outside your tents.

ODYSSEUS

What stopped him from murdering us?

ATHENA

I stopped him, made him hallucinate,
diverted his eyes from his desire.
I turned him on the herd
and the guards posted on watch.
He jumped in striking at horns,
severing spines in circles around him.
He thought he killed the Atreids
and was attacking some other generals.
I made him sick with rage,
drew him tighter in the net,
and soon the work exhausted him.
He tied up anything still alive
and led them to his tent
thinking oxen and rams were men.
He has them trussed for torture.

Let me show you this sickness
so you can tell the Greeks.
Stay calm. He cannot harm you.
I will make his vision dim;
he will not see your face.

You there, with the prisoners inside,

put down those ropes a moment!

Ajax, come! Step outside the tent!

ODYSSEUS

What are you doing, Athena? Don't!

ATHENA

Quiet—stop being such a coward.

ODYSSEUS

No, he's fine where he is.

ATHENA

Why? He is just a man.

ODYSSEUS

Yes, but I can't stand him.

ATHENA

Isn't it sweet to mock him?

ODYSSEUS

I'm happy enough with him inside.

ATHENA

Are you afraid of his raving?

ODYSSEUS

Sure, I wouldn't be afraid otherwise.

ATHENA

He cannot see you, even nearby.

ODYSSEUS

He still has eyes, doesn't he?

ATHENA

I will wrap him in darkness.

ODYSSEUS

I guess gods *can* work tricks.

ATHENA

Now be silent and stand still.

ODYSSEUS

Fine, but I'd rather be gone . . .

ATHENA

Ajax! I have to call twice?

This is how you treat friends?

AJAX

Hail, Athena! Hail, daughter of Zeus!

My ally.

I'm just about to

crown your altar with these spoils.

ATHENA

Excellent news.

But tell me this:

was your weapon aimed at Greeks?

AJAX

Yes! Proudly. I won't deny it.

ATHENA

And did you attack the Atreids?

AJAX

They won't insult Ajax ever again.

ATHENA

So I gather you killed them?

AJAX

Dead.

      Let them steal weapons now.

ATHENA

Well then, what about Laertes' son?
Did he get away from you?

AJAX

Want to know about that bastard?

ATHENA

Yes—Odysseus, your nemesis—tell me.

AJAX

My favorite prisoner is inside, goddess.
I won't kill him just yet.

ATHENA

Why not? What are you doing?

AJAX

First, he's tied to a post . . .

ATHENA

And then? What will you do?

AJAX

. . . then whipped bloody . . . *then* he dies.

ATHENA

You go a little too far.

AJAX

Whatever else pleases you I'll do
but he gets what he deserves.

ATHENA

Since you seem to enjoy yourself,
go—let your mind run wild.

AJAX

Back to work.

Grant me this:
that you fight beside me . . . always.

ATHENA

See what gods can do, Odysseus?
Who was more sane than Ajax?
Did anyone act with better judgment?

ODYSSEUS

No.

I feel sorry for him
even though he's still no friend.
He's completely out of his mind
and that could easily be me.

If you stare hard at life
you see we're nothing but shadows.

ATHENA

Take a good look and learn.
Do not brag to the gods.

Never be arrogant because you think
yourself stronger or richer than anyone.
One day can change it all.
This is human life.
Gods love
the wise but hate a fool.

∎

CHORUS
a child
the ocean
Salamis silt sea bed

if it were different
god could strike again
the Greeks tell lies
he seems as wary
as a dove's eye

the night now shot
dawn astounds from tomorrow

while crazy horses wander
the meadows kill Greeks
root and branch

a breath draws under
the zodiac of fire
listens to whispers billow

Odysseus' necklace of ears
hears what he says
the fool will imagine
his own better ending
in which you die

the price of fame
even the dead ask
who won't believe it

he once was lucky
seemed to rise up
held on the shoulders
of his adoring enemies

buoyed by their screams
it's beyond you now
to make out voices
in all the noise

stop him from shouting
it can't hurt much
when the eye shuts
you'll hear birds call
it will only open
to a vulture's menace
and a silent throat

Artemis fond of bulls STROPHE
the story goes
it's such a shame
pushed on the milling herd
she's jealous that you cheated her
of some prize
false
    ungifted
        on the hunt

or was it bronzebodied War?
the spear lays blame nightly
disgrace makes its plan

out of your mind
Telamon's good boy
to hack at cattle
inspired my boy really inspired
rumor and Zeus and Phoebus refuse
if by sham
two kings allege you mythic
the image of Sisyphus' kin
don't don't *stay inside sir*
or the rumor fits

on your feet
you're off balance
while you stagger on the sidelines
an idiot makes headlines
so easy and so arrogant
a walk in the park
make them hysteric

you'll laugh someday if
you survive the pain

TECMESSA

Friends of Ajax, shipmates,
tribe of earthborn Erechtheus,
all of you homesick
for Telamon's distant country,
I have painful news:
massive, powerful Ajax
is sick and troubled.

CHORUS

what does day swap
for night's weight?
Teleutas had a child
you're that shotgun concubine
Ajax took and favors
what you could tell

TECMESSA

Where do I start?
It hurts to say.

"*The*" Ajax is insane—
he raved all night.
He's in the tent
caked in dried blood.
His victims speak volumes.

is it starting to clear himself?
he'll outrun you the brutal truth
a story's as famous as
the men who tell it
it's easy to see where this is headed
kill him with frantic hands heap
cattle and minders in
a black stinking pile

From—*there*—he came,
leading by tether animals
whose throats he cut
and ribs stove in.
He took two rams,
severed tongue then head

from one, the other

he strung up

and used a harness

to whip it senseless,

cutting and cursing it

like a man possessed.

now it closes hoods the head

theft of feet that can move

to thrash for an oar

dropped from a quick ship

the double Atreid plied threats mount and break

Ares just a stone's throw off

get away from him

he'll take you under

TECMESSA

Enough—it's over now.

The storm has calmed,

but sanity is painful.

He sees the mess

—no one else's fault.
That's hard to take.

but if he's over it's good
the spell passes and doesn't matter

TECMESSA

I don't know which I'd pick:
hurting while my husband enjoys himself
or misery for both of us.

CHORUS

double up woman it gets better

TECMESSA

He's no longer sick—he's worse.

CHORUS

how is it what you say?

TECMESSA

At least while he was sick

he was happy in his havoc;

I was the one in pain.

But after he could breathe again

the ugly truth poured over him.

I'm no better now than before

and his problems have just doubled.

CHORUS

you're right

             must be from god

struck so

             even after it goes

he's no better off than crazy

TECMESSA

But that's how things stand now.

CHORUS

where does bad luck fly from?

tell your story   share the grief

TECMESSA

Here's as much as I know:
in the middle of the night,
after the fires died, he rose,
armed, and began to go out.
I nagged him and I said,
"What's the matter? There's no alarm,
is there? Where are you going?
The entire army is still asleep."
He gave me that old line:
"Woman, silence makes women more beautiful."
He obviously wanted to be alone.
I don't know what happened outside
but he returned leading a mob
of hobbled bulls, dogs, and sheep.

He began to break their necks . . .
slit their throats . . .

                        cut their spines . . .
some he tied up and tortured.

He went outside ranting at phantoms,
talking to nobody about the Atreids

and Odysseus, breaking into scary laughter,
bragging how he'd make them pay.

But after he came back in
he slowly began to regain sense.
He looked around, saw the wreck,
started beating his head and shouting.
He sat down among the carcasses
and began pulling at his hair.

After he was silent a while
he finally spoke and threatened me
if I didn't tell what happened.
He asked what he had done.
I was afraid to say anything
but told him what I knew.
He began to shake and cry.
I've never seen him that way.
He's always said that only cowards
and the weak show their emotions.
The most I'd heard from him
was a bull's groan—heavy and low.

Now he sits in there dazed.

He won't eat or drink anything,

surrounded by those butchered animals,

                                        motionless.

He's going to do something bad.

He's moaning and muttering to himself.

That's why I came out here.

I need to get him help,

friends who can calm him down.

CHORUS

Tecmessa tells a terrible story

the man's been inspired by evil

AJAX

No! No! No!

TECMESSA

It's going to get worse soon.

Do you hear Ajax? That shouting?

AJAX

No! No! Noooooooo!

CHORUS

either he's sick or he's seen
what he's done in the night

AJAX

Where's my son?

TECMESSA

God!

He's calling for you, Eurysaces.

Where are you?

What's he want?

AJAX

Teucer!

Where is my brother, Teucer?!

He's wasting time while I'm suffocating!

CHORUS

he's in control   let him out
the daylight will sober him up

TECMESSA

Open it. Look,

        see for yourself

what he's done—

        did to himself.

AJAX

Ha!   STROPHE

Sailors—my only friends—

it's apt you're here.

See how just now

a wave of blood

broke all around me.

CHORUS

she's got it right it seems
the matter's out of his mind

AJAX

Agh!   ANTISTROPHE

My crew of sailors

who churned the water.

You're the only ones

who can end this:

please, just kill me.

well spoken

   sensible

      pile it on

can't take it? then kill it

AJAX

Look at me: huge,   STROPHE

strong, fearless in combat.

I murdered *farm* animals.

I'm nothing but a stupid joke.

TECMESSA

Stop it—don't talk that way.

AJAX

Still here? Why haven't you left?

Fuck.

   FUCK!

TECMESSA

It's done.

Now stop talking nonsense.

AJAX

Idiot.
I released
the ones responsible,
hacked at spiral horns
and pretty herds of goats.
I'm drenched black.

CHORUS

why do you worry the past?
it can't be what it isn't

AJAX

It's all clear now.   ANTISTROPHE
Laertes' son, the tool,
the army's biggest bastard,
enjoys a good laugh on me.

CHORUS

only god gives laughter and wailing

AJAX

I'd just like to find him.

Damn it!

CHORUS

keep talking you'll make it worse

AJAX

Zeus, my ancestor,
how can I
kill that fool and
the two brothers, our kings,
and then die?

TECMESSA

You're asking for my death too.
How could I survive without you?

Heh.

Bright oblivion—

hell shines for me.

Come take me home.

Take me! I'm not fit

to call on some god

or even see another day

now that Zeus'

daughter, harsh goddess,

has ruined me.

Where to run?

Where to stay?

My life ended,

friends . . .

with these animals

on a useless hunt.

Now the entire army

clenches fists.

You're pathetic.

You say things now
that you would never tolerate before.

Agh!
Rushing water,
tidal caves, and thickets
for far too long
have covered me at Troy
without once letting me breathe.
Anyone with sense could see.
By the Skamander
and nearby streams
malignant to Greeks
not one man
has there been
—write it down—
of all those
armed at Troy,

no one matched me.
And now I lie
in shame.

CHORUS

can't stop what he can't talk
he's fallen in a bad way

AJAX

Now when people hear my name
what will they think?
                              A catastrophe.
"Ajax' Catastrophe" has a nice ring.
I'm a double, no, *triple* disaster.
My father came here to Ida.
He was decorated for his courage.
He brought fame home with him.
Here's his son, the same place,
just as strong as he was
and I'm no less a soldier.
I've become an embarrassment to Greeks.

But I do know this much:
if Achilles had awarded his arms
he would have picked the strongest;
no one would have cheated me.
The generals planned this with Odysseus;
they pushed me to the side.
If I'd kept my eyes open
and hadn't been distracted, there wouldn't be
awards like that with rigged votes.

Then Zeus' daughter, hard, glaring Athena,
she took me by the hand
and led me stumbling into sickness.
I washed hands in cow blood
while my enemies ran away laughing.

It wasn't by choice.
                    But when
gods get involved, winners become losers.

What now?
                    The gods hate me.

That's obvious.

                So do the Greeks.

Even this Trojan dirt hates me.

What if I leave the harbor,

sail across the Aegean, go home?

How will I look at him—

Telamon?

            How will he see me?

I'll be naked without self-respect.

He wears success like a badge.

I couldn't take it.

            Then what?

Back to the front by myself?

Do something heroic and get killed?

But that would please the generals.

No.

     I can find something better,

a way to show my father

that his son's not a coward.

Longevity is ugly for a man

if life doesn't get any better.

What pleasure is there in days
that just stretch out to death?
I wouldn't give a single cent
for a life filled with delusions.
Either live well or die well;
that's all there is to it.

CHORUS

no longer the instrument of another
Ajax your mind is your mind
so take some advice from friends
if you can't think they can

TECMESSA

Ajax, there's nothing you can do.
There's never anything anyone can do.

I was born free, my father
as powerful as anyone in Phrygia.
Now you hold title to me
and you make all my decisions.

You took me.

                I accepted you.

Please, Ajax, for our home's sake
and for the bed we share,
don't leave me to your enemies.
Don't make me follow another man.
Because when you die or disappear,
I know on that same day
I'll be dragged away by Greeks—
along with your son—into slavery.
I can hear what they'll say:
"Well, look at her—Ajax' woman.
He was the army's champion once.
Now she works for the competition."

They'll taunt *me* like that, yes,
but *your* family will be shamed.
You'll disgrace your father, growing old
back home.

                You'll disgrace your mother.

She's seen her share and often
prayed that you would come back.

But think of your son, Ajax.
He won't have a proper upbringing,
an orphan without real family.

What's worse?

That's what your death would do.

I don't have anyone but you.
You took my father from me.
Life dealt my mother different cards,
but death caught her as well.
I have no home but yours.
No livelihood—my salvation is you.
Please think of me.

A man

should remember if he enjoyed himself.
Favors deserve a favor in return.
But if he can't remember kindness,
what kind of man is he?

CHORUS

it's a pity Ajax a pity
her word wants its own approval

AJAX

You can count on a favor
if you do as I say.

TECMESSA

Say it, Ajax, I'll do it.

AJAX

I want to see my son.

TECMESSA

He's not here . . . I was afraid . . .

AJAX

During the commotion? Is that it?

TECMESSA

Yes, I didn't want him hurt.

AJAX

I would have done the same.

TECMESSA

But, just in case, he's safe.

AJAX

Good.

      You did a wise thing.

TECMESSA

How else can I help you?

AJAX

No, I want to see him.

TECMESSA

He's nearby.

      A servant's watching him.

AJAX

Then why don't you bring him?

Eurysaces, your father's calling.

                        Bring him

and put him into Ajax' hands.

AJAX

Is he coming?

            Didn't they hear?

TECMESSA

Here they come.

            Here he is.

AJAX

Bring him.

           He won't be afraid
of the weapon or the blood,
not if he's truly my son.
It's the rough rules I follow;
he has to be broken in.

Hope you're luckier than I, boy.
If you're like me otherwise, good.

Right now I'm a little jealous:
you don't know what's going on.
Life's sweet when you know nothing,
before learning to celebrate or regret.

When you reach manhood show them—
our enemies—what you got from me.
Until then breathe the clear air,
grow up, be your mother's delight.
Greeks won't do you any harm
even when I'm no longer around.
I'll leave Teucer to guard you.
He'll raise you, keep you safe
once he returns from the fighting.

All you soldiers and sailors here,
I'll ask a favor of you.
Give the following instructions to Teucer:
take the boy to my home,
show him to Telamon and Eriboea,
have him care for my parents
until they meet the god below.

No judges will award my equipment
to others, not to my rivals.
But you, son, take your namesake,
Eurysaces: Broad Shield.

                     Hold the strap—
seven unbroken folds of taut oxhide.
Bury my other arms with me.

Here, quick, take this kid away.

Seal up the house.
                 No crying.
Stop being so damn sentimental, woman.
Cover up.

          Good surgeons don't pray
when it's time to start cutting.

CHORUS

desire can be a deadly thing
the tongue's a blade that threatens

TECMESSA

What do you plan to do?

AJAX

Don't ask.

Self-control is best.

TECMESSA

My blood's cold.

For Eurysaces' sake,

for god's sake, don't do this.

AJAX

You're starting to whine too much.

And when have gods helped me?

TECMESSA

Don't blaspheme.

AJAX

Tell someone who cares.

TECMESSA

Won't you listen?

AJAX

I've heard enough.

TECMESSA

I'm afraid, Ajax.

AJAX

Shut the doors!

TECMESSA

God, calm down.

AJAX

Don't be stupid.
You know me better than that.

■

home is somewhere else
the good island beats
its head above water
far where the long time absence
suffering on the plain of Troy
the months flow by
uncounted and worn
with false hopes
that escape to the place the pit forgets

Ajax gets in line
behind the other problems
that room with madness
was quick in the way before
now his mind an empty field
where friends find hurt
at his hands
his best gift
not friends they fall they fell like kings

was old as a day is
in your mother's white head when

the mind eats
alone alone alone
is not the nightingale's bird anguish
is her sharp-toned song of unluck
drum the chest
to kept time
thump and tear her hair out

that hidden in hell is better
than the best of his race
of struggling Greeks
fed on anger
steady it was but now wanders
shame father when you learn it
the disturbed child
who's grown schizophrenic
come of age in the family

AJAX

All of everything—it never ends.

Secrets emerge and facts are buried.

Eventually nothing should surprise.

Time breaks

our promises and our strong will.
Once I withstood anything that came,
like steel. I've lost my edge
thinking what would happen to her,
widowed, orphaned child, left to enemies.
I'll go wash by the shore
and clean this filth off me
now that the sickness has passed.

I'll go to a trackless place
and I'll cover this ugly weapon,
bury it where no one sees.
Night and hell can have it.

I took it with this hand
from jinxed Hector as a gift—
I got no prize from Greeks.
But what they say is true:
an enemy's offering is no gift.

I'll give the gods the future
and learn respect for the Atreids.

They rule—I submit.

                         What else?

Every strong thing has to fade:
the coldest winter, thick with snow,
makes way for a lush summer;
the stretch of worst night ends
in the white dazzle of day;
there are winds that can calm
any groaning ocean; and even sleep
in time must release its prisoners.
What else could we reasonably think?

For me, I've learned well that
you should hate only so much—
enemies become friends.

                        And a friend
you should help only so much.
No one stays by you forever.
Companions will give you false shelter.
In the end it works out.

Go in, woman, and pray that
the gods grant what I seek.

And my friends, respect my wishes.
Tell my brother when he comes
to care for me and you.
I'm going where I have to.
Do what I say.

                       Soon you'll
hear that my problem is solved.

■

CHORUS

prickle and shake nervous and high   STROPHE
yo-ho Pan's here Pan
walk on the water
climb on the ice
up over the rocks
dance like a god
Mysia style Cnosos style
let go the mind and spin
he dances he knows
over the Icarian Ocean

comes the lord Apollo
he is made visible
he is present he is glad

Ares draws dread from the eye
and now again yo-ho
now the sharp white
gleams in day's light
as a fast aircraft
Ajax lifts off weightless
and obeys natural selection
kills his victim by the book
time eats it all
don't repeat the unsaid
it's such a surprise
Ajax altered in mind
he finds a path to peace

MESSENGER

You folks, I've got some news:
Teucer, just come down from Mysia,

was going back to the garrison
when the Greeks started insulting him.
They recognized him as he approached
and formed a circle around him.
When they had him completely surrounded
they said his brother was crazy.
No way he would have survived.
They were set to stone him,
tear him apart.

They would have.
Weapons were drawn; they were ready.
But at the very last second
senior officers talked sense into them.

Where's Ajax?

He needs to know.
I have a message for him.

CHORUS

not in there   just went out
latched on to a new plan

MESSENGER

Oh no,

Teucer was too late sending me . . .
or I didn't come fast enough . . .

CHORUS

what could be all that bad?

MESSENGER

Teucer said he *must* stay inside.
Don't go out until he arrives.

CHORUS

departed
        he picked his best option
to settle up with angry gods

MESSENGER

. . . the stupidest thing he could do . . .
if what Calchas says is true . . .

what could you know about it?

Here's what I know so far:
the generals had called a meeting.
Agamemnon, Menelaus—they were all there.
But Calchas left to tell Teucer
he should do whatever he can
for the rest of the day
to keep Ajax inside his tent,
otherwise he'd never see him again.
He said Athena would harass Ajax
for just a single day—today.

If you boast about your strength
the gods will knock you down.
The prophet said Ajax is human
and he stepped out of bounds,
said when Ajax was leaving home
he ignored some good advice.
His father said, "Plan to win

with weapons, but god gives victory."
And Ajax' answer, arrogant and asinine:
"Father, with gods' help even nobodies
can be powerful. But I'm different.
I can be famous without them."
Big words.

       Then a second time
in battle Athena came to him
urging him to kill the enemy.
He had the gall to say,
"Queen, go help some other Greeks.
I've got things under control here."
Gods hate that kind of thing.

He's outrageous and she got angry.
But if he can survive today
we'll save him—with divine help.
That's all the prophet could say.
As soon as Calchas told him,
Teucer sent me to warn Ajax.

But it's over if he's right . . .

CHORUS

Tecmessa burns and is born unlucky
she'll see the threat he says
so close it shaves the skin

TECMESSA

It's been quiet for a while
but it isn't finished, is it?

CHORUS

listen to this man just arrived
news of Ajax that will sicken

TECMESSA

You have bad news for me?

MESSENGER

Don't know about you . . .

                but Ajax . . .

if he's outside . . .

            I'm afraid so.

TECMESSA

He's out.

What are you saying?

MESSENGER

Teucer sent me to keep him
inside and not let him out.

TECMESSA

Where's Teucer?

What did he say?

MESSENGER

He's coming.

If Ajax goes out,
Teucer thinks something bad will happen.

TECMESSA

Oh no.

How does he know?

MESSENGER

Thestor's psychic son.

Calchas said today
brings life or death to Ajax.

TECMESSA

Friends, you have to stop this.
Quick, tell Teucer; bring him here.

Split up—go east and west.
We've got to find Ajax.

I shouldn't have let him go.
He tricked me.

He doesn't care.

No, I won't just sit here.
Even I'll search where I can.
Let's go.

Quickly, we're wasting time

. . . and he's in a deadly hurry.

ready to go

        talking's all done

down to business

        time to run

■

AJAX

The killer is cocked and ready—
and if I think about it,
a gift to me from Hector
who was my most hated enemy—
planted in the angry Trojan ground.
It's armed.
      It's aimed.
          It's hungry.
Everything rests on the trigger's edge.
It'll do this last quick favor.
It's all set—so am I.

First, I pray to you, Zeus,
but I won't ask for much.

Just send word about what happens
to Teucer so he finds me,
fallen here over this bloody weapon,
before my rivals get to me
or dogs and birds eat me.
Only that, Zeus—all I ask.

Hermes, show me the way below.
No struggle—just a quick jump;
finish this all in one shot.

Next, I call on the Furies
who see all of human pain,
awful inescapable demons.
                    Look at me:
the Atreids destroyed me at last.
Share some of this with them.
If they get to watch me
killed here by my own weapon,
let their families feed on them.
Hurry and take revenge, lightning sisters.
Enjoy them all—spare no one!

You, driver of the sheer sky,
Sun,

   when you see my home
slow down just a little bit
and tell them my sad story.
Tell my father and unhappy mother.
My miserable mother . . . when she hears
she'll be screaming in the streets . . .

Enough daydreams.

      It's pointless to grieve.
I've got a job to do.

Death!

   Death, come look at me:
you and I have some business.
And you, blinding fire of day,
one last time I'll salute you,
but this is it—never again.
The light,

    the land,

      the world,

Salamis,

       the place I called home,
and Athens

       and all the people,
springs and rivers

       and even Troy,
goodbye to everything that fed me.
I've said my last to you;
the rest I say in hell.

CHORUS

hurt heaps hurt here
left right
left where it will
will it learn the place?
dropped it
dropped can't find it be found
half a boat's oars in sync
with what?
beach to the west is stippled
by tracks
that fade like sores fill eyes
when stares the sun so much
it's plain what follows the man

who can it see

blind fish in caves

or owls in the mountains or

rivers in flood?

where's a raw mind

wanders and glances?

the wishes the distance

who can escape it

a race in the wastes

as feeble as he is now?

TECMESSA

No, no, no!

CHORUS

what shrill calls from the dark?

TECMESSA

Why did you—?

CHORUS

stare down the barrel my dear

the gaping accusation makes no sound

TECMESSA

It's over.

It's done.

I'm dead.

CHORUS

what's it over?

TECMESSA

Ajax killed by his own weapon,
his body wrapped around a secret.

CHORUS

there's no home gone
you've killed it sir
the sailing the suffering
the woman in pain

TECMESSA

How do I keep from screaming?

CHORUS

whose was the hand of disaster?

TECMESSA

He killed himself—

                the weapon's buried,

propped here under his slumped body.

CHORUS

rash soaked in blood

and ignored

no one says or sees

forget it

       where

          where

does stubborn

Ajax unluckily lie?

TECMESSA

He can't be seen like this;

I'll cover him with my coat.

No one should have to see

the blood coming from his nose,

the black weapon, and this wound.

Who will help me lift you?

Where's Teucer?

He should be here.

He should bury his brother's body.

Ajax, to end up this way . . .
even your enemies will stop short.

bound he was bound
to do something stupid
angry obsessed the fit wouldn't quit
night and day
eaten raw with hatred
the Atreids goaded
it's a deadly position
a good long time
since he entered the struggle
that had started a game ago

No, no, no!

CHORUS

you feel it in your stomach

TECMESSA

No, no, no!

CHORUS

say it again it won't change
what you love is gone woman

TECMESSA

You can't imagine what I feel.

CHORUS

so it seems

TECMESSA

Everything's closing in on us, Eurysaces,
no one to watch over us.

CHORUS

yes double the hurt
you echo the unspeakable
an ache of Atreids
if god won't protect

TECMESSA

Something supernatural took hold of him.

CHORUS

it's heavy so heavy it is

TECMESSA

The daughter of Zeus did this.
She turned a favor for Odysseus.

CHORUS

his intent is black
patient man
he's crazy with success
laughs and laughs yes
with two kings
there listening

TECMESSA

They'll laugh, joke at this wreck
since they never wanted him alive.

They'll call when the fighting starts.
Fools.
       They'll soon learn the value
of this man they threw away.

Bitter for me;
               for them—sweet;
for him—peace.

             He got what
he wanted.
        He wanted to die.

They can't take credit for this—
the gods did it, not them.
Odysseus can brag all he wants.
Ajax can't hear him.
        He's gone.
. . . Grief is all he left me.

■

TEUCER

Oh no! No!

CHORUS

silence

　　　Teucer has something to say
he shouts a song of recognition

TEUCER

Oh, Ajax, my brother . . .

　　　　　　　my brother . . .

it's not a rumor . . .

　　　　　it's true . . .

CHORUS

see for yourself

　　　the man destroyed

TEUCER

Why did this have to happen?

CHORUS

it just did

TEUCER

It's all over.

CHORUS

groan over again

TEUCER

Finished so fast.

CHORUS

too true Teucer

TEUCER

God, the mess.
But his son—where is he?

CHORUS

the baby's alone

Quick, get him!
Bring him here.

The lion's gone—
don't let someone steal the cub.
Go! Get him!

It's too tempting
now that his father is dead.

CHORUS

it's what he wanted while alive
everything worked out just as planned

TEUCER

My eyes have seen ugly things,
but nothing as painful as this.
Nothing else I've had to do
has made me feel so sick,
Ajax, as when they told me
I needed to find your body.
That news cut like god's voice.
They said that you were dead.

I started shaking from far off.
Now seeing . . .
                    I can't control it.

Oh god.

Go ahead—
                    pull back the cover.

The face of a determined man.

Now I pay off your debts.
What man will help *me* since
I was no good to *you*?
Or Telamon, your father and mine,
think he'll look kindly at me
coming home without you?
                    Not likely.
He rarely smiles when he's happy.
What name won't he call me?
"The bastard he got by force,"

x

"Coward,"

        . . . the failure who abandoned you,
Ajax . . .

        Or that I planned it
so I could take your inheritance.
Or anything.

          Age makes him bitter.
He just wants to argue anymore.
He'll throw me into the street—
by rights—more slave than free.

That's at home.

        Here at Troy,
many enemies and very little help.
That's what your death leaves me.

How do I get you off
this filthy weapon?

        The fucking thing
opened you up.

        Who would expect

Hector, who's dead, would kill you?
Look how you both ended up:
with the belt you gave him
Hector was bound, dragged, and mangled
until the corpse released his spirit.
From him you took this gift
that delivered your own final annihilation.
Didn't a Fury forge this weapon?
Wasn't that belt made in hell?
I say it's always the same:
gods plan these things for humans.
Whether you like it or not,
I don't care.

        I'm done talking.

CHORUS

don't carry on

        cover him up
get to the point my boy
look someone hateful on the way
full of schadenfreude and ill wishes

TEUCER

Who's the man coming from camp?

CHORUS

Menelaus whose problem launched 1,000 ships

TEUCER

I see who it is now.

MENELAUS

Listen here, don't touch that body!
Put it down.
                    Leave it be.

TEUCER

On whose authority are you acting?

MENELAUS

Mine, on behalf of the army.

TEUCER

Then tell me, on what pretext?

This: when we launched we believed
Ajax was an ally and friend.
Evidently he's worse than the Trojans.
He would've murdered the entire army,
was armed, had it all planned.
Had not god quashed the attempt
I'd be where he is now,
lying there dead in public shame.
He'd be alive.

          But god intervened
and turned his violence on sheep.
Consequently, there's not a man alive
with the authority to bury him.
He'll lie fallen on the beach,
food for sea birds and crabs.
That's that.

          Get used to it.
Maybe we couldn't control him alive,
but he'll follow our orders now.
Like it or not, he's ours.

He just wouldn't listen to me.
It's typical of the common herd
never to listen to their superiors.
Our cities would decay into anarchy
without the real threat of punishment.
No army can be run well
without bulwarks of fear and shame.
A big man ought to understand
small vulnerabilities can bring him down.
If you have awe and humility
you know how to save yourself.
Immorality and license in a city
are fine while the weather's fair,
but over time it will decline.
Give me reverence and order anytime
over indulgence in whatever gives pleasure
without any regard for the consequences.

But what goes around comes around.
He burned hot—now *I* do.
And I'm telling you: no burial
. . . unless you'd like to join him.

it sounds so sensible Menelaus but
show some respect for the dead

TEUCER

Gentlemen, why should I be surprised
that an ordinary person makes mistakes
when leaders—from good families apparently—
can say the most stupid things.
Come on.

You led Ajax here
and brought him as your ally?
Didn't he come on his own?
When did you ever command him?
How do you rule his people?

You rule the Spartans, not us.
Nothing gives you any more claim
to order him than he you.
You came second in command anyway,
not general of the entire army.

Go yell at your own men.
You and your brother can howl.
I've got a funeral to prepare;
I'm not afraid of your mouth.

Ajax didn't fight for your woman
like the poor bastards you brought.
He had an obligation under oath—
he wouldn't fight for just anybody.

Come back with a bigger entourage
and bring Agamemnon if you like.
I'm not impressed by the noise.

CHORUS

not good to talk that way
the truth has teeth you know

MENELAUS

Marksmen talk tough but stay hidden.

TEUCER

A marksman's skill shouldn't be underestimated.

MENELAUS

What you'll say from behind cover.

TEUCER

I'll face you in the open.

MENELAUS

Your tongue stokes a good fire.

TEUCER

Because I know when I'm right.

MENELAUS

It was right to kill me?

TEUCER

Kill?

You manage to keep talking.

MENELAUS

God saved me, despite Ajax' intentions.

TEUCER

Then don't disrespect your divine savior.

MENELAUS

How will I break divine laws?

TEUCER

If you don't allow him burial.

MENELAUS

No, he declared war against me.

TEUCER

When did Ajax ever confront you?

MENELAUS

You know we hated each other.

TEUCER

You rigged a vote against him.

MENELAUS

The *voters* rejected him, not me.

TEUCER

You sure made it *look* legal.

MENELAUS

You're starting to piss me off.

TEUCER

Oh really?
Welcome to the club.

MENELAUS

I'll say one thing: no burial.

TEUCER

Hear this: he *will* be buried.

MENELAUS

I once knew a real loudmouth
who wanted to sail in winter.
When the weather started getting rough,
he didn't seem quite so talkative
and was much easier to tolerate.

Your yammering reminds me of him.
We just need a little storm
to get some quiet around here.

TEUCER

I once knew a fool myself
who enjoyed seeing other people hurt.
One day, somebody resembling me,
with a temper like mine, said,
"Don't insult the dead, my friend,
if you do, you'll regret it."
Right to the unfortunate man's face.
You remind me of that man
quite a bit.
                You get it?

MENELAUS

I'm leaving.
                I'm embarrassed to talk
when I ought to beat you.

Get out of here.

I'm embarrassed

to listen to an idiot's bullshit.

now you've done it

if you still can

cover him up quick

time that a hero

returns to the dirt

Here they are, just in time—

the man's woman and his son

come to pay their last respects.

Come here, boy, close by him,

kneel and pray by your father.

Take my hair that I've cut

and we'll cut some of yours—

so—like a suppliant.

If soldiers

try driving you from the body,
may they die and lie exposed,
uprooted and severed from their families
like these strands of our hair.
Stay and watch over him, boy.
Kneel beside him and touch him.

You men, stop acting like women.
Fall in!
   I'm going to scout
a gravesite
     . . . even if it's illegal.

■

CHORUS

where will it end
the count of the years wandering
the toll the statistics of missiles
in flight that fall
back to the ground
where a crater accuses

better hurled into space
or into the crowd in hell
than to be a bomb maker
and share your results
the Los Alamos boys
knew what they'd done

they ended the party
the glass is empty
the guests have gone
and the music has just stopped
now he lies awake in bed
alone, no one to hold him
still in his clothes
the bed soaked
his hair matted
he's got to forget

what sleeve slid back
to show the nightmares
where Ajax lay exposed?
demons crawled out of the dream
and ate him   ate his soul

left his scattered remains on Greenland's
ten-thousand-year-thick sheet of ice
he's slowly melting
into the ocean
home calls to him

TEUCER

I thought I better head back
when I saw Agamemnon coming over.
Get ready.

   He's going to unload.

AGAMEMNON

The courier brought a disturbing report
that you were mouthing off disrespectfully.
I'll remind you of your rank:
your mother was a war trophy.
You act like she was royalty.
You're nothing standing up for nobody.

You claim we aren't the commanders
of the Greeks or of you,
that Ajax came on his own?

Big talk coming from a slave.

Who's this man you're shouting about?
Did he fight anywhere I didn't?
Are there no Greeks but him?

I regret ever suggesting that contest
to award the weapons of Achilles.
I have to listen to you.

You can't see that you've lost
and just accept the majority's decision.
Like every sore loser you insult
and make excuses for your failure.
If I let this go on
we'll lose all respect for order.
If legal victories are always overturned
why not give everyone a prize?
No.
        Not while I'm in command.

The most powerful man is nothing
without self-control and mental discipline.

A big ox can be led
by a very small nose ring.

I've got a remedy for you
if you don't regain your senses.
Ajax is just a shadow now,
yet you talk like he thrives.
He can't protect you anymore, son.
You better get yourself some help
if you want to face me.

What's the use?
                    Discussion is over.
I don't understand your babble anyway.

CHORUS

you both should get some wisdom
best advice there is for you

TEUCER

How quickly a man's memory fades.
The respect he's earned deserts him.

He has no regard for you,
Ajax, with your memory still fresh.
You risked your life in combat;
that's all garbage to him now.

What you say makes no sense.
Do you remember anything?
                              Remember when
you were boxed behind your barricades?
The enemy had overrun your position;
they poured in from all sides;
the stern decks of some ships
had already begun to catch fire;
Hector himself had crossed the trench.
Who turned them back?
                              This man.

Whom you say you stood beside?
Did you approve of *that* behavior?

Or when he faced Hector alone?
In the lottery for that mission

he didn't use a heavy marker,
some mud clod.

He carefully picked
one that jumped from the helmet.
He wanted to go

. . . with me,
the slave son of a *barbarian*.

Are you out of your mind?
Perhaps you're not aware your grandfather,
Pelops, *Phrygian* king, was a barbarian.
And your own disgusting father, Atreus,
fed his brother his own children.
Your mother (from *Crete*) was caught
by your father with a foreigner.
He drowned her with mute fish.
And you talk about my family?
I am the son of Telamon
who was highly decorated in combat.
My mother, she was a queen,
daughter of Laomedon.

She was chosen

by Heracles as a special prize.
I come from two good families.
I'm not ashamed of my blood,
blood which you forbid a burial.

It's you who should be ashamed.
Listen carefully: if he lies here
we three will lie beside him.
That's a better cause, I think,
than to die for your wife—
no, excuse me—your *brother's* wife.
Do yourself a favor and listen.
If you make trouble for me
you may regret being a hero.

CHORUS

commander Odysseus come just in time
your tangling may still untie this

ODYSSEUS

What is it? From way off
I could hear your voice, Agamemnon.

AGAMEMNON

Did you hear the insulting language
this man was just using, Odysseus?

ODYSSEUS

How's that?
     He's got a right
to respond if he's being abused.

AGAMEMNON

He only gets what he deserves.

ODYSSEUS

So how has he offended you?

AGAMEMNON

I forbid any funeral for Ajax.
He threatens to bury him anyway.

ODYSSEUS

Can I speak frankly with you
without doing harm to our friendship?

AGAMEMNON

Go ahead.

I'd be a fool

not to listen to my friend.

ODYSSEUS

Then listen: for god's sake yield.

Don't make this man lie unburied.

Don't let your anger control you

so hatred steps on what's right.

Just like you, I've resented him

since we competed for Achilles' weapons.

But even so, that's not enough

to defame him or to deny

that he was the best fighter—

except for Achilles—here at Troy.

It's not right.

You'd be violating

not just him but divine law.

It's wrong to dishonor a soldier,

even if he did oppose you.

So you're on his side too?

I hated when hate was justified.

But dead, he doesn't deserve abuse?

Don't gloat, Agamemnon, it's beneath you.

It's not easy to be commander.

Then rely on a friend's advice.

Maybe *you* should do the listening.

Stop! Concede this—you've already won.

AGAMEMNON

Do you remember who you're helping?

ODYSSEUS

A rival—but he was noble.

AGAMEMNON

Why then?
You pity your enemy?

ODYSSEUS

The man's valor trumps my hatred.

AGAMEMNON

Men like this one are unstable.

ODYSSEUS

Anyone can turn fierce then friendly.

AGAMEMNON

You endorse this kind of friend?

ODYSSEUS

I *don't* endorse a hard head.

AGAMEMNON

You'll make us look like weaklings.

ODYSSEUS

To Greeks we'll be acting justly.

AGAMEMNON

So I should permit this funeral?

ODYSSEUS

Yes. I'll need one myself someday.

AGAMEMNON

It's all the same.

Suit yourself.

ODYSSEUS

Yes, I serve myself.

Why not?

AGAMEMNON

It's your project—leave me out.

ODYSSEUS

However it happens, you deserve credit.

AGAMEMNON

Fine.
　　　But understand: it's a favor
I do *you* because you asked.
Either on earth or in hell
I loathe him.
　　　Do your duty.

CHORUS

who says you're not cunning Odysseus
must be a very stupid man

ODYSSEUS

Teucer, I want to make amends.
I stand here as your friend.
I've come to bury the dead,

to help you with the funeral
as is due to a soldier.

TEUCER

Odysseus, thank you for the offer.
I didn't expect this at all.
You hated him more than anyone.
Yet you're the one who helps,
who wants to honor his memory,
unlike that shell-shocked general of ours
and his loudmouth brother.
                            They wanted
Ajax to lie without a tomb.

I hope Zeus, who accomplishes all,
and the Furies, who never forget,
punish those bastards for this attempt
to disgrace Ajax without good cause.

But you, son of old Laertes,
I'm reluctant to let you handle
the body or join the funeral.

Pay your respects in other ways.
Anyone can—I have no problem—
but burial I'll arrange by myself.

I see you're a decent man.

ODYSSEUS

I just wanted to help you,
but I respect that.

                    I'll go.

TEUCER

Enough.

            Time is wasting.
Go, dig a grave.
Draw him a bath
to wash him as
we ought.

You, to the tent,
go get his weapons.

Escort your father, boy,
touch him like me;
help us carry him.

The wound still blackens . . .

Come, all you friends,
stand to.
                Move out.

Was a good man!
There was none better,
I say,
            than Ajax!

CHORUS

who sees can know
but no one sees
next
        about
            to be

AN ACCOUNTING

Ajax is odd. To be sure, any Greek tragedy is an alien thing for a modern reader, with its shocking violence, obscure religious themes, and stark formality. Yet even in this peculiar world, *Ajax* sticks out. It seems designed to contradict itself. The protagonist meets an abrupt and unexpected end while the drama itself—just as unexpectedly—continues without him. It is a play of profound spectacle—the goddess Athena appears— and lurid display—a bloodied madman raves and then commits suicide on stage. The tragedy begins with dignified and moving poetry and then the language degenerates into petty insults and seemingly pointless bickering. Odysseus opens the action, declaring his hatred for Ajax, but arrives at the close to offer aid to his former enemy. When I first read the play more than twenty years ago it struck me as absurd.

Now, however, I read it as a story of inversions. Ajax kills himself with a weapon given to him by his enemy, Hector, to seal a truce. This token of friendship proves lethal for its recipient, an irony mentioned three times in the play. Ajax first draws attention to the fact in his cornerstone speech at lines 646–92 where he goes on to enumerate a list of inversions: winter turns to summer; night yields to day; enemies become friends, and friends betray. This central message, that almost anything eventually transforms into its opposite, plays out in the very structure of the tragedy itself. With the death of Ajax the world becomes in Bernard Knox' words "a smaller, meaner place" and the play then undergoes a near total cast change. Ajax is replaced by his half brother, Teucer. Tecmessa, the strong woman, is replaced by the effete Menelaus. The divine power of Athena is replaced by the temporal authority of Agamemnon. In each case a noble individual makes way for an attenuated copy. Only the changeable Odysseus keeps his place on stage. Yet he enters the drama as Ajax' antagonist and returns at the end as an ally. The play culminates at its center with the hero's suicide, and folds these reversals around that event.

My formal decisions preparing the translation are also somewhat unusual but apt, I suppose, given the curious nature of the play. This translation uses a counted line. That is, the length of each line is determined by the number of words in the line. Further, I have constrained the number of words per line to match the number of metrical feet found in the Greek. Sophocles used a six-foot iambic trimeter line (two feet per metron) for the spoken passages of the play. Consequently, in rendering the speeches, I use six words to the line. The choral and lyric passages of the Greek text vary in line length, but once the measure is set for a strophe, its paired antistrophe uses the same structure. My choral passages do likewise. The translation has as many lines as does the original in the Oxford Classical Text I used. Essentially I have taken the play into English at an exchange rate of one English word for every metrical foot in the Greek.

At the start I toyed with using a seven-word line; seven is a comfortable length for me and one I use in many of my own poems. But the Greek itself wanted something faster. The six-foot line of the original immediately suggested a six-word English line.

That length gives the speeches noticeable velocity and conveys a better sense of what goes on in the Greek. Sophocles can be startlingly elliptic. Greek's multiple oblique cases, verbal moods, and myriad tenses allow him to say more with fewer words than English requires, and he takes full advantage of all the linguistic machinery at his disposal. The six-word line suggests some of the compression and rate of Sophocles' dialogue. It is, in the end, impossible to do in English what he can do in Greek. But the short line helps keep up with the rapid and dense original, and pacing is a central concern of this translation. Translations of Sophocles are often faithful yet prolix. There is an urgency in *Ajax* that demands brisk movement. Ajax' drive toward self-destruction, the fractious exchanges over his body, and the sharp criticism of war that undergirds the entire play all argue for energetic pacing. Admittedly, my line is shorter than Sophocles'—I overcompensated to emphasize the rate. But I start with the premise that a translator has to run faster in English to keep up with Greek. Once I had settled on the six-word line for the speeches, I had a rule—one word per foot—that suggested itself for the lyric passages.

I now had my measure, but when I used it on the
choral sections my first efforts were unsatisfying.
The pace set by the word-per-foot rule seemed right;
that was not the problem. Rather, the language of the
chorus itself in my early attempts lacked the energy of
the original. Sophocles moves into an entirely different
register when the chorus sings. His normal voice in the
speeches is very economical and in the lyric interludes
he takes the poetry into new levels of gnomic density.
The language becomes torqued, often involving convo-
luted syntactic constructions. The overall effect is one
of tightly strung poetry in which individual stanzas are
tense from end to end. Naturally, these parts of his
plays present the most difficult challenge to a transla-
tor. My rendering of the spoken sections hews fairly
close to the Greek but it quickly became clear that the
chorus needed something different. I was not capturing
the tonal and energetic shift from speech to lyric. Here
I took cues from two other poets, Christopher Logue
and Louis Zukofsky.

Christopher Logue's account of the Iliad, *War Music*,
is for me one of the most exciting versions of Homer
to appear in recent years. Logue is unabashedly igno-

rant of Greek but this handicap proves an advantage since it makes him fearless in his use of anachronism to convey the emotional sense of the original (if not its literal meaning). He deploys cinematic stage direction, machine guns, and Antarctic geography to startle the reader and refresh the poem. Alternatively, Louis Zukofsky's homophonic translation of Catullus (*"odi et amo"* becomes "O'th'hate I move love") offers an approach that is less about semantics than capturing the formal effects of the original. With these two radical approaches in mind, I attempted to push my treatment of the choral passages into new territory. I listened to the Greek and tried to incorporate the alliteration and repetitions of Sophocles' poetry and even a textual lacuna. I also decided to improvise on the literal meaning to capture the emotional content of the source. The chorus in any of Sophocles' plays acts as a running commentary on the events of the drama and sets the tone for each scene. *Ajax* concerns itself with madness, so I decided to turn the chorus into a kind of disturbed unconscious to the play itself. This involved two deliberate distortions. First, I eliminated any use of first person in the chorus to disembody it. And second, I exaggerated the psychological elements and distressed the syntax into a slightly disjointed raving. The result is a sinister, nagging voice that punctuates the action.

Like all of Sophocles' tragedies, *Ajax* has a moral force. But this play has a particularly urgent message for those of us today in Britain and the United States who find ourselves victorious but powerless after our own misguided adventure into the Near East. *Ajax* demands our attention, not only for its clear-eyed account of the bitter aftermath of victory but also for its treatment of unscrupulous politics. Accordingly, I have tried to find modern equivalents for certain terms and images. This was not an attempt to bring the drama into our time but rather to employ language that would resonate with my contemporaries. Throughout I have used my own American idiom and have worked to produce a translation that would be natural for modern actors to perform.

Clearly, I have taken liberties. What then is lost in this translation? As Robert Frost would say: the poetry. Sophocles' poetry has been replaced by my own. A poem is a very particular thing made from very particular material at a particular point in time. The word *translation* bears the unfortunate Latin root of "carry across," when in fact so much can never leave the original language. Instead, I see poetic translation as a kind of forgery. It is akin to building a copy of a house seen across a river. We cannot ferry the house over to our side and cannot even cross the river to get a close look at it from all angles. We have to stand on this bank, examine it from what vantage we have, and reconstruct the house with materials at hand. I am, in the end, uncomfortable being called a translator. I prefer what Sophocles would have called me: ἑρμηνεύς—interpreter.

A NOTE AND

ACKNOWLEDGMENTS

Line numbers at the feet of pages correspond to
those used in the Oxford Classical Text of Hugh
Lloyd-Jones and N. G. Wilson, on which this transla-
tion is based. Because that text realigns earlier manu-
scripts yet keeps the prior numbering, it falls out of
step in several passages.

Like every other English-speaking reader of Sopho-
cles in the last century, I am deeply indebted to Richard
Jebb. I relied heavily on his *Ajax* commentary and, to a
lesser extent, W. B. Sanford's commentary on the play.

Excerpts from the translation previously appeared
in *Chicago Review* and on the web at *Cordite Poetry
Review*, *Fascicle*, and *MiPOesias*.

I'd like to thank my employer, Morningstar Inc.,
whose progressive policies include a six-week paid

sabbatical for every four years of service. A large portion of this translation was drafted during one such break.

Finally, I am obliged to note the assistance of a number of people who commented on earlier versions or helped me read the play in public performances. Special thanks to Andrew Blom, Amina Cain, Eric Elshtain, Devin Johnston, Michael O'Leary, Peter O'Leary, Mary Margaret Sloan, John Taggart, and David Wray. All of you contributed more than you know.

our Key to a Future in the Travel Tourism Industry

GLOBAL TRAVEL
TOURISM CAREER OPPORTUNITIES©

g.e. Mitchell

Author, Tour Designer & Lecturer

Global Travel-Tourism Career Opportunities

TAKE OFF!
Let a 25 year expert be your guide into the travel-tourism industry
and help you map your career in travel-tourism

Learn "Inside Secrets" ~ Where the high paying jobs are
Turn your hopes into action!
Learn How to turn your avocation into vocation
Learn The Secrets of a good "Resume" for success
Learn How to start your own travel-tourism business
Find Career Peace and Satisfaction

Copyright 2005
Gerald E. Mitchell

A "How To" Guide for thousands of people who
Want to discover the world as a career

Global Travel Tourism Career Opportunities©

By

Global Travel Tourism Career Opportunities©

© Copyright 2006 by The GEM Institute of Tourism Career Development
www.tour-guiding.com

First Edition: March, 2006

Library of Congress Cataloging Publication Data
Mitchell, Gerald
The GEM Group
ISBN 0-945439-14-8

Inquires should be addressed to:

The GEM Group, Ltd.
P.O. Box 21199
Charleston SC 29413
Email: gerry@tour-guiding.net
http://www.tour-guiding.com

The GEM Group, Ltd. Institute of Travel-Tourism Career Development

The GEM Institute of Tourism and Career Development evolved from the travel professional's demand for unique and innovative material.

Overseen by Mitchell, these publications continue to surpass other competitive literature and are setting higher standards for the travel market.

Mitchell's works are currently in use in the United States, the Middle East, the (former Soviet Union) New Independent States, the Caribbean Basin, Canada, Latin America, Serbia, and Russia.

Continued international growth is imminent as the world's hunger for Mitchell's consulting talents take him around the globe.

The mission of the Institute focuses on preserving the unique history, culture, and ecology of the region that is being promoted to the traveling public.

The promotion of these countries natural resources helps to stimulate the economy while preserving the ecological balance of nature and visitor.

The GEM Group, Ltd.
Established 1976

*A company dedicated to helping countries develop
a successful and profitable tourism destination*

A full service Tourism and Travel firm, the GEM Group Ltd. Was established in 1967 with the initial purpose of operating as an International Tour Operator company.

Since its founding, the firm has expanded its services from specializing in high-adventure tours to include Hospitality and Tourism Training, Tour Product Development, Marketing and Tour Guiding throughout the world.

Specializing in Cross Cultural Transfer, Rural and Ecotourism product development and marketing, The GEM Group, Ltd. provides the necessary training required for increasing long-range productivity by meeting product demand delivery services while ensuring viable and sustainable economic benefits to the client.

Mr. Mitchell, President of The GEM Group Ltd. and his staff of seasoned travel professionals conduct lectures in t Mr. Mitchell also has authored numerous travel and tourism texts currently in use throughout the world.

The GEM Group Ltd. established the first indigenously owned and operated outfitter and guide service in the Canadian Arctic.

The GEM Group Ltd. Professional Affiliations

- Registered with Who's Who National Registry
- Member of the Society of Travel and Hospitality Executives
- Organizations of American States (OAS)
- World Bank—IMF, DACON
- Lecturer for the Small Business Resource Center
- GEM Manuals registered with the Library of Congress
- GEM Publications are sold through Barnes & Noble, Books-a-Million, and Borders
- US Commerce Department (SABIT), Washington, DC
- Trainer for Russia and New Independent States of the Former Soviet Union
- Unite States Agency for International Development
- Jordan—United States Business Partnership
- USAid-Booz, Allen, Hamilton, Belgrade, Serbia

Acknowledgments

I would like to express my gratitude to the many students around the world who encouraged me to write this book. They provided important information, and made hundreds of helpful and often candid comments. Too numerous to mention here, they include over 23 countries, NGOs, United States Agency for International Development, the Organization of American States, the Canadian Government, and other Ministries of Tourism and observers.

g.e Mitchell
Author, Tour Designer & Lecturer

Gerald E. Mitchell, President
The GEM Group, Ltd.

Table of Contents

- *Sector Two: Tourism Providers*
  Special Events, Conferences, Convention Planning
  Nature Guiding Careers
  Outdoor Adventure Guides
  Guides and Pro-Instructors for Ski Resorts
  Fishing Lodge Guide and Instructor
  Riverboat Rafting Tour Guide
  Historical, Cultural Interpretative Guides
  Museum Curator Tour Guides
- *Sector Three: Working for Government, State & City Tourism Boards*
  Convention Sales Manager
  Tourism Marketing Coordinator
  Visitor Information Counselor
  Working for the National & State Parks Service
  State and Regional Park Ranger ~ "Smoky the Bear"
  City Parks Recreational Programmer
- *Sector Four: Welcome to the Transportation Field*
  Motor Coach, Rail, Cruise Lines, Airlines
  Motor Coach Driver/Charter Local Sightseeing Conductor
  Director of Sales & Marketing for Charter Motor Coach Companies
  Rail Service, Amtrak, North America
  Railroad Engineer
  Railroad Conductor
  Jobs in the Cruise Industry
  Passenger Service Representative
- *Sector Five: Airline Careers and Employment Opportunities*
  Airline Pilot
  Flight Attendant
  Airline Reservationists
  Customer Service Representatives
- *Sector 6: Theme Parks and Attraction Centers and Broadway*
  Attractions Ride Operator
- *Sector 7: Alternative Paths to Your Dream Job*
  Travel Writer Photographer
  Teacher/Trainer for the Hospitality-Tourism Industry
  Yacht Crew-River Boats
  Ski & Spa Industry

Career Opportunities and Resorts & Sopas

Choosing the Ski Industry as a career

Choosing the Spa Industry as a Career

New Age Retreats Careers

Become a Private Pilot or Start Your Own Business

E-Commerce Travel Careers

What Attracts You to the Travel Industry

Chapter 4: Owning Your Own Travel-Tourism Business 63

- Are You an Entrepreneur at Heart?
- Life Changes
- Assuming the Role of a Self-Employed Owner/Manager
- First Business essential: Prepare a Comprehensive Plan
- When Can You Expect to Start Making Money?
- Prepare a To-Do List in Your Startup Planning Stage
- Seven Profitable Business Opportunities
- Owning a Boat Charter Company or Being a River Boat Captain
- Visitor Accommodations
- Hotels
- Bed and Breakfasts and Farm/Ranch Vacation Sites
- Cabins, Cottages, and Houseboats
- Campgrounds
- Catering to Travelers who Want to Shop
- Visitors Need to Be Fed!
- Providing a Tour Guide Service
- New Business Opportunities
- Heritage Interpreter
- Tour Guide Adventure Tours
- Starting an In-Bound Destination Management Company
- Designing and Escorting Tours for the Physically Challenged
- Career Opportunities for International Tour Directors
- Five Key Considerations in Tour Promotions
- Becoming a Dream merchant
- Questions and Answers About the Travel-Tourism Industry

Message from the President of The GEM Group

Gerald E. Mitchell, CEO & Founder of the Institute of Travel-Tourism

My goal is to speak to you personally and share knowledge from my past and present experiences as a travel-tourism professional for the past twenty-six years.

The information I'm sharing is intended to help launch your career in the Travel-Tourism industry. Each section of this book will provide you with "inside secrets" to finding a career or staring your own business in the Travel-Tourism industry. One of the great appeals of the this industry that it is competitive, challenging and also fun!

Your opportunities for employment in travel-tourism are growing at impressive rate! By 2007, an additional 130 million new tourism jobs will be created around the world with over 400 different type of employment in careers that range from adventure tour guides to caterers to hotel managers to travel agents. Tourism is one of the fastest growing industries in the world today. An exciting career awaits you if you enter travel-tourism now!

Chapter 1

Welcome to the Travel-Tourism Industry

What is Tourism?

Although many of us have been "tourists" at some point or another in our lives, we seem to struggle for the words when asked to define what tourism actually is ...

> **Tourism** /tüe(r)izm/ *n.* the temporary movement of people to places
> other than work or home, the activities undertaken during their stay
> and the facilities created to meet their needs

The World's Fastest-Growing Profession!

Because the industry has been experiencing a boom time, we are in desperate need of qualified tourism professionals. Tourism is one of the few industries that can offer exciting, challenging and varied careers -- *plus fast promotions!*

> The travel-tourism profession currently employs one in ten people worldwide.

Tourism benefits both developed western nations and emerging third-world countries. Tourism creates jobs and boosts the local economy. Visitors support the economy by spending money in shops, in local transportation, at hotels and restaurants. Tourism is a key source of civic pride. It pays for regenerating old building sites and museums and helps with local conservation and environmental improvements.

New Jobs and Business Opportunities Are Waiting for You!

Manufacturing exports have declined in the United States, while service industries such as travel-tourism are contributing more and more to the world economy by means of "invisible exports." Travel-Tourism professionals gather components such as hotel accommodations, dining, and transportation and put them all together to create a tour. The tour is then sold to tourists either through the Internet, travel agents, or tour operators. As more and more manufacturing jobs continue to be exported overseas, our tourism service is contributing more and more to our country's prosperity.

Selling Tours for Profit

A "tour" is an intangible product. The tourist cannot touch it, take it home and try it out for a week, the send it back if it fails to please. Once purchased, the sale of a tour is final. Therefore, the overall quality of each tour is vital to the continued success and development of any travel destination – and to the tour operators and agents who sell them.

How Exporting Tourism Works

Each year, the Caribbean countries export tons of bananas – a tangible product -- to the U.S. and Europe. If U.S. and European residents decide to visit the Caribbean as tourists, they are receiving an "intangible" service during their visit as tourists. These services include transportation, hotel rooms, admission fees to attractions, and other expenses. Now multiply the average spending per tourist of $350 per day by the thousands of visitors each year, and you can see how tourism is a thriving industry contributing to the world's economic health. Today travel tourism earns more in foreign currencies than any other industry.

Competition For Tourist Dollars

All countries compete for the tourist dollar! The majority of countries compete in a global market to attract tourists from the United States, Japan, France, and many other countries.

With the aid of advertising and promotional firms, directors of tourism often implement aggressive and creative marketing campaigns aimed at attracting travelers from other parts of the world.

Eight Essential "Pulling Powers"

Traditionally, local resources are incorporated into visitors' tour itineraries by airlines, hotels, travel agents, tour guides, museums, and national parks. These resources become tour features and highlights.

#1- Service: YOU can play an important role in the set of tourism resources by delivering one or more of the tourism-travel services for transportation, accommodations (hotels and resorts), tour guiding, tour operations, catering, bars/clubs, street vendors, ethnic cuisine – plus the basic services all tourists may need, from working in currency exchange offices to providing medical services to working in government tourism offices.

#2- Local resources: A destination's resources are what appeal to the visitor. The tour features form the core of the visitor's attractions, including accommodations, food, shopping and entertainment. Tour features include natural and man-made attractions at the travel destination.

#3- Cultural Resources

Religious: mosques, temples, churches, cathedrals, missions, pilgrimage sites, burial grounds

#4- Natural Resources

Flora: **Wild flowers, wilderness, coffee plantations, spices & herbs, vineyards, jungle**

Landscape: **beaches, caves, coral reef, volcanoes, gemstones, desert**

Fauna: Birds, insects, wildlife, marine mammals, wild game

Climate: Four seasons, summer, fall, spring, and winter

Water: rivers, springs, oceans, ice, snow, waterfalls

#5- Heritage: castles, forts, historic birthplace, historic buildings, historic homes, cottage, ghost towns, folklore, museums-monuments, battle sites, ancient roads or paths, aboriginal, indigenous, landmarks

#6- Event Resources:

Festivals: music-jazz, folk, country, classical, ballet, national

Tournaments: sports-local, regional, athletics, racing, horses, dogs, camels

#7- Business: trade shows, agricultural, business, social clubs, conventions, carnivals, fishing, and ethnic celebrations

#8- Activity Resources:

Ski Lodges- Scuba Centers-theme parks-Zoos, art & crafts courses-outdoor activities which could include class at, golf courses and not to be overlooked Shopping!

 The Tourists are coming! Are you ready?

There are two types of tourism: inbound and outbound. Each of these offers opportunities for your career.

Outbound Tourism

Outbound tourism is the type with which you may be most familiar. It involves the business of people going from their country to another -- for example, leaving one's home and going abroad is considered *outbound* tourism.

Inbound Tourism

When tourists from other places visit your country or community, this activity is referred to as *inbound tourism.* Many people in work as travel-tourism professionals dedicated to ensuring that inbound tourists enjoy their stay and will want to recommend your country "as the place to visit" when they return home.

Five Stages of a Visitor's Travel

Stage 1: Pre-Departure

Travelers have many concerns before they depart, and these concerns can affect their choice of destinations. Typically, tourists ask:

- Is it safe to travel on my own?
- Is the destination and the tour package a good value?
- What if I don't know the language?
- Will the trip meet my expectations?

The tour director is a primary resource for ensuring the travelers' needs are met.

Stage 2: Arrival

Traveling to the destination, experiencing jet lag, facing culture shock with first impressions, standing in line, being welcomed and greeted, having safe and reliable transportation

Stage 3: The Visit

The tour guide is the person to whom travelers look to see that the services that were agreed on are provided, that they receive information, and that the tour runs smoothly. A successful tour guide will have great people skills, and be able to satisfy complaints and resolve misunderstandings. Tourists expect:

- ☑ Lodging at clean locations with good service
- ☑ Dining at interesting restaurants with international cuisine
- ☑ Entertainment, learning experiences, and native culture
- ☑ Shopping, unique gifts, arts and crafts
- ☑ Recreation (eco-tours, heritage, cultural, special interest programs)

Stage 4: Departure:

At this stage, visitors will be forming final impressions and looking forward to the trip home.

Stage 5: Post-Tour-Memories

Tourists will tell their friends how good or bad the experience was. Their word-of-mouth recommendations will either sell others on travel or discourage them. This stage is the one where they are most likely to register complaints for poor service.

Chapter 2

Your Career in Travel-Tourism

Seven great Reasons for a Travel-Tourism Career

#1.   World's largest employer

#2.   World's fastest growing industry

#3.   With over 7 sectors of the industry, you'll find a exciting job that suits your interests

#4.   You can have fun while associating with people on vacation looking for a good time

#5.   Global opportunities to travel and work around the world

#6.   Be proud to be a host for your country or region, showing it off

#7.   Each day is different, offering new opportunities and challenges

Unlimited Career Paths and Opportunities

The diverse career paths in travel-tourism show that your options are virtually unlimited. Depending on your interests and skills, you can work indoors or out, nine to five or midnight to noon. You can work in an office, an airport, or out of your home. You can have one career in the winter and another in the summer. In short, you can make your career fit the lifestyle you want!

One of the great appeals of careers within the travel-tourism industry is the opportunity for motivated people of all ages and backgrounds to move up the career ladder rapidly or even to own their own hotel or travel firm. Lack of experience is no barrier to employment or advancement in many tourism and hospitality careers. Many company executives started out as hourly workers and are now managing large hotels, transportation firms, or even bringing their family members into their own company.

Special Note: The economics of the 21st century will be dominated by three industries: telecommunications, information technology, and tourism. The travel and tourism industries have grown by 500% in the last 25 years. By 2007, it is estimated that tourists will spend $884 billion in foreign countries and on tourism related activities.

Getting Started: Overcoming A Lack of Experience

You will need to focus on your objectives and convince a potential employer that even if you do not actually have industry experience, you understand the fundamentals and are motivated to learn and make the travel-tourism your career choice.

You will not only advance in your career based on seniority and day-to-day skills but also based on a well-planned career blueprint that you can share with your employer. Taking additional courses and attending workshops will improve your knowledge and skills and enhance your opportunity to transfers these skills to other jobs where there will be additional responsibilities and salaries. Remember, the lack of experience is no barrier to employment or advancement in the travel-tourism industry.

Many fields do require specialized training and education beyond high school. Your education within the travel-tourism industry can be enhanced by attending two-year and four-year colleges, vocational/technical schools, and universities. Travel-tourism offers year-round workshops, seminars, and site-inspection (FAM) tours to help you move into higher management positions.

Entering Travel-Tourism as a Front-Line Employee

Many people in tourism careers start in front-line positions. These positions generally involve direct contact with customers and often require people to work together as a team to meet customers' needs and expectations.

Experience

Management and human resource executives seek individuals who have a professional manner, attitude, and appearance. This is important because the business survives if customers' needs and expectations are met, and one of those expectations is approachable, congenial, helpful staff. In addition, each position always requires its own set of job skills -- those specific skills required to do the job you are hired to do.

In some tourism positions, it is possible to learn these skills on the job. For other positions, such as Motor Coach driver or Interpretive Guide, employers may offer extensive training before you begin to work on your own. Still other front line positions, such as Travel Agents/Tour Operators-Tour Director (for incentive and special interest groups), require prospective employees to have the necessary training and skills before they are hired.

Conditions

Many front line positions may require shift work. Some positions are seasonal, offering more hours during peak season, and then perhaps changing employees' positions or temporarily reducing staff numbers as the low season approaches. For the right people, these criteria make positions of this type perfect. A nine-to-five job does not appeal to everyone. So if you like variety, the freedom to finish work early or start work late in the day, and/or time off seasonally or periodically so that you can take courses or travel, front-line positions may be ideal for you.

Rewards

Salaries for front line positions may start at minimum wage or at the lower end of the wage scale. However, for many positions, salary is supplemented with gratuities, commissions and/or discounts, or complimentary products or services. In addition, large businesses or chains often have more opportunities for growth and advancement. Smaller companies, however, generally offer more diversified job descriptions, enabling an employee to try a variety of tasks and learn a variety of skills. Both situations can allow you to expand a résumé or prepare for ownership of your own small business.

Flexibility

Career choices in the travel- tourism industry offer *flexibility*. You may start out as a travel agent and change to hotel management or start your own adventure touring company. The enormous scope for movement among the industry's many and varied sectors is a vital consideration in view of many jobs becoming obsolete or being shipped overseas.

The Hours

Very few jobs within the tourism industry are nine-to-five. There will be occasions when you will be called upon to work weekends and holidays. Criticism has been that the travel-tourism profession that it involves working long, often unsocial hours. The industry does require a strong personal commitment for those very reasons. However, fast promotion, financial remuneration, and job satisfaction outweigh the abnormal working hours.

Salaries

Salaries may differ from country to country. Moving up the ladder of success, you may start out as a front-line worker, then move on to a be a supervisor or manager and then into an executive position. The tourism industry moves fast; there is the constant turnover (advancement, transfers) and retirement, leaving openings for ones who have demonstrated a professional attitude and aspirations to make tourism their career choice.

Check travel web sites or talk to a person already in the tourism industry concerning what you can expect the pay scale to be in your career choice. Also, attend travel/tourism industry trade shows, and be sure to refer to contacts located in the resource section in this book, which provides sample salary ranges in different professions. Please note that these are *averages* and are subject to change. Many jobs in the tourism industry offer perks such as accommodations, meals, and bonuses based on production and of course... *TRAVEL!*

There are many benefits beyond salary to starting as a front-line employee. You will gain:

- operational skills

- communication skills

- customer service skills

- product knowledge

- company knowledge

- interpersonal and teamwork skills

- and much more, depending on the sector and position that you have chosen.

Your immediate boss or manager will be on the lookout for those employees who are motivated and show an interest in a company or a position. Turnover can be high in some sectors, positions and regions, so your movement to another position or career path category could be swift if you exhibit the necessary attitude and desire.

Here is a brief monthly overview of the OPPORTUNITIES NEWS & TRENDS in the Travel—Tourism Industry!

What's' going on in the Travel-Tourism Industry Today?

By permission from the May 2005 *Travel Career Connexxions Opportunities* newsletter

WTTC Unveils 2005 Travel & Tourism Country Forecasts

So just how well is the global travel industry faring this year? The World Travel & Tourism Council (WTTC) last week released its 2005 Travel & Tourism forecasts for 174 countries at the 5th Global Travel & Tourism Summit in New Delhi, India. Releasing forecasts prepared on its behalf by Oxford Economic Forecasting, which follow the United Nations standard for Tourism Satellite Accounting, the WTTC reported that the record robust recovery started in 2004 should continue through 2005 at a healthy rate. WTTC also reported that the December 2004 tsunami, which struck some tourism destinations around the Indian Ocean, had a significant, but limited overall impact on the tourism economies. Worldwide for 2005, WTTC is forecasting the following. Demand for all components of Travel & Tourism consumption, investment, government spending and exports is expected to grow 5.4 percent (in real terms) and total $6.2 trillion in 2005. The 10-year annualized growth (2006-2015) forecast is 4.6 percent per annum illustrating the outlook for strong long-term growth. The continued strength of the pound and Euro against the U.S. dollar is expected to push visitor exports to nearly $820 billion in 2005 or real growth of 7.3 percent. Travel & Tourism's contribution to the world economy is illustrated by the direct industry impact of 3.8 percent of total GDP and the combined direct and indirect impact of the Travel & Tourism economy expected to total 10.6 percent in 2005.

The global Travel & Tourism industry is expected to produce 2.1 million new jobs in 2005 over its 2004 level to total 74.2 million jobs or 2.8 percent of total world employment. The broader perspective of the Travel & Tourism economy (direct and indirect) is expected to create more than 6.5 million new jobs for the world economy for a total of 221.6 million jobs dependent on Travel & Tourism or 8.3 percent of total employment. Said WTTC President, Jean-Claude Baumgarten: "We turned the corner in 2004 and it's full steam ahead for Travel & Tourism in many countries and regions around the world.

The WTTC also released its 2005 Top Ten List of Travel & Tourism economies. For the second year in a row Montenegro has placed first as the fastest growing Travel & Tourism economy in the world. India and China placed second and third respectively illustrating the impact of the emerging middle-classes has on Travel & Tourism growth. In order, the top 10 are Montenegro, China, India, Croatia, Sudan, Vietnam, Laos, Czech Republic and Guadeloupe. For more information, visit www.wttc.org.

Never Traveled Abroad?

There are great opportunities to expand your horizons waiting if you are willing to "test the waters" by working in developing countries, especially where rural eco-tourism is growing.

Source for additional information:

- Global Routes: Globalroutes.org
- Global Works: globalworksinc.com
- Putney Student Travel: www.goputney.com
- Visions Service Adventures: visionserviceadventures.com
- Where there be dragons: www.wheretherebedragons.com
- World Horizon International: world-horizons.com

Do You Have What It Takes To Work in Travel Tourism?

Of course, the very best way to determine whether a career in travel tourism is right for you is to work in the field for a few years and explore the many opportunities. However, there are certain characteristics that help assure success. On the following page is a test of the traits desired in travel-tourism workers that may help you decide.

What You Need to Succeed In Travel-Tourism

How Is Your Attitude?

Essentially, tourism is a people-oriented business. Whether you work directly with customers or behind the scenes, their satisfaction, safety and enjoyment is the number one concern. Tourism is also dynamic and competitive. The ability to constantly adapt to customers' changing needs and desires is important to successful tourism businesses.

Characteristics of a Successful Travel-Tourism Professional

Do you have the necessary characteristics?	Comments:
Pleasant, "Can-Do" Attitude	Ability to find solutions to problems
Good communication skills	Articulate, able to talk easily in front of a group
Education for at least entry-level job	Start with a high school diploma
Ethical and honest	Trustworthy
Reliable	Can be counted on to do your job without supervision
Friendly	Outgoing, able to make new friends easily
Patient	Willing to tolerate difficult people and situations
Tactful	Can negotiate without antagonizing others
Consistent	Steady, dependable
Enthusiasm	Real enjoyment of work
Pride	Delivers the best work performance under all conditions
Leadership/persuasion	Can lead a group effectively
Good at helping /instructing other	Enjoys teaching and helping others to learn about new places
Problem-solving/creativity	Can find solutions to complex problems
Work as part of a team	Able to work effectively with others
Frequent public contact	Enjoys working with the public
Manual dexterity	Can organize luggage, assist tourists with physical problems
Physical stamina	Able to work long hours at a stretch
Be willing to go out of your way to help visitors and your co-workers	*Most of all! Must be a good team player!*

Chapter 3
Where the Jobs Are: Travel Industry Sectors

Six Industry Sectors ... *Plus One More!*

Exciting career opportunities can be found in all six travel-tourism industry sectors:

Sector 1: Retail Travel Agency

Opportunities include working as a tour operator at an in-bound destination management company. You can even travel the world *FREE* as an international tour director! For in-depth information about this career, see Gerald Mitchell's book, *How to Travel FREE as an International Tour Director*.

Sector 2: Special Events, Conferences, and Convention Planing

You can be a tour guide for adventure tours or eco-tourism outdoors. Professional Tour Guides work at showing tourists special heritage events and sites. Interpretative Guides provide information on cultural sites and museums, even serving as museum curators.

Sector 3: Government and Local Tourism Boards

Convention Sales Managers, tourism marketing coordinators for state visitor information bureaus, and Information Counselors at National and Sate Parks are popular career choices in this sector. Some find careers as park rangers or City Parks and Recreation programmers.

Sector 4: Transportation

Railways, motor coaches, and other transportation lines provide career opportunities to work in reservations, ticketing, conducting, and being the engineer/operator. Many rail lines and coaches offer jobs as tour guides who accompany passengers on trips.

Sector 5: Airline Careers

You don't have to be a pilot to enjoy the opportunities to travel and work with airlines. Flight attendants, reservationists, security personnel, and baggage handlers are needed, too.

Sector 6: Theme Parks and Entertainment

Imagine a day at Disneyland without anyone to operate the rides, handle guest services, or serve food – or to play the vital role of Mickey Mouse and other Disney characters. Theme parks offer positions that require acting ability, marketing experience, and management to keep the parks running smoothly and the guests happy.

Industry Sub-Sectors

There are two subcategories in the travel trade sector. The first is the *retail* arm of the industry, made up of travel agencies. The second is the *wholesale* side, made up of tour operators, who sell packaged tours to travel agencies.

The travel-tourism trade sector supports the bookings and sales in other sectors. The people that work in the travel trade make reservations for accommodations, tours, transportation, food and beverage service, and/or for attractions. These bookings can be in the form of an all-encompassing tour package or a single booking for a single traveler.

Stimulating career opportunities continue to grow to include working for airlines, cruise ship companies, leisure or corporate travel agencies, tour operators, and Internet travel companies. The employment picture is excellent for all those interested in acquiring the necessary skills, including mature persons and those seeking re-entry or second careers. As an entry-level employee you may start taking bookings on behalf of tour operators, sell cruises, make hotel reservations, receive payments and give advice on travel destinations, passports, visas, and foreign currency. You'll need to have good knowledge of the tour products and destinations offered by the tour operator.

Travelers seek out professional travel agents, tour operators, and tour guide services to help with information gathering and planning their vacation or business trip. Budgeting, special interests, transportation, and safety are some of their main concerns for these clients. Today's traveler may seek a traditional packaged tour, a program which can range from several days to three weeks. The trip may cover North America or a number of countries in Eastern Europe. Aside from offering traditional tour packages, cruises, hotel accommodations, and transportation, the travel company will be required to supply additional information regarding visas and medical requirements for travel abroad.

Among the many employment opportunities in the retail sector are:

- Retail Travel Agent
- Tour Operator/Wholesaler
- In-Bound Destination Manager (IDM)
- Travel FREE as an International Tour Manager/Director
- Special Events and conference planner
- Professional Tour Guide for historic sites, nature tours, and adventure touring
- Incentive Travel specialist
- Sales and Marketing
- Tour Promotions manager
- Package Tour Coordinator
- Owner/Manager

The Retail SubSector ~ **Careers at Retail Travel Agencies**

Overview: Travel agencies sell travel packages as well as individual travel components, such as airline tickets, car rentals, and hotel reservations. They sell directly to the public, to both business and pleasure travelers. With the increase of ticketless travel, web marketing pages, Internet Exchange and E-commerce (which allows for electronic billing and payment), many small travel agencies are entering alliances with other agencies or with large agency consortiums. This allows for increased buying power through shared purchases of technology, management systems, and training.

On the Job Duties and Responsibilities: Typical responsibilities include selling vacation packages; making reservations for business travelers; interpreting complex schedules and brochures for the client; computing fares and issuing tickets; preparing invoices, vouchers and other office forms; and providing travel information by researching resource materials. The travel consultant must have a strong interest in various cultures and in world travel. He or she should be able to function under pressure, pay attention to detail, and enjoy working with people. Professional travel agents gain valuable information through tourist offices, reference books, web sites, guidebooks, trade publications, brochures and through familiarization tours and cruises. Among the duties at travel agencies are:

- Sales and marketing
- Calling on fraternal, religious, or social organizations
- Participate in "FAM" tours- familiarization study trips
- Familiar with configurations of airplanes and cruise ships
- Ticketing procedures for planes, trains, cruise ships, tour programs, car rentals and hotels

The Wholesale SubSector ~ **Careers as Tour Operators**

Overview: Tour operators are involved in planning, development, promotion, administration, and implementation of tourism products. They oversee all the day-to-day tasks and also supervise, motivate, and train staff. They are employed by tour or transportation companies, resorts or attractions. They may travel to proposed tour sites, check them out, and experience the services first-hand before assessing their tourism potential.

Duties: Tour operators and wholesalers develop and package tours to sell to the retail trade; i.e., travel agencies. Often these tours are all-inclusive (they include all travel, accommodations, meals, and entertainment) and are marketed to encourage specific tourist markets to buy. For example, they sell employee incentive travel; and convention-related or special interest travel, such as theatre, sports or bird watching tours. Some tour operators specialize in tours to international destinations; others focus on groups coming into North America.

Tour operators work independently or are affiliated with an airline, motor coach line, or other travel-related business. They respond to changes in the industry by developing new and unique products that have a competitive edge in price, value, and variety. Both retail and wholesale operations employ many people in a variety of positions. This is a competitive industry, and new regulations (for example, airline deregulation), industry consolidation and new packages to new destinations keep those who work in this sector busy and challenged.

Experience: Management and tourism experience, human resource management skills, leadership and team-building skills, and financial management skills are all required. Good communication and excellent customer service skills are also necessary. Knowledge of relevant destinations, attractions and travel are important, as are research skills. Desired experience and skills include a second language, risk management skills and time management skills.

Wholesale SubSector ~ **In-Bound Destination Management**

"Dream Merchants" is the name sometimes applied to tour operators who manufacture tours. Their duties include putting the different travel components together, researching and developing tours, creating new ideas, and marketing the tour programs. Domestic tour operators may be smaller scale and more narrowly focused than international tour operators, but in many cases they offer greater growth and more career opportunities.

In many respects, domestic tour operations affords greater creativity because there are so many more markets for domestic tour products than for international ones, and the industry has really only begun to tap these resources. Indeed, domestic tour operations has in a sense been reborn, and newcomers to the field have a chance to be in on the ground floor. The Destination Management Company (DMO) Operator/Owner/Manager should have strong management and tourism experience, human resource management skills, leadership and team-building skills, and financial management skills. Good communication and excellent customer service skills are also necessary. Knowledge of relevant destinations, attractions, and travel are important, as are research skills. Desired experience and skills include a second language, risk management capability, and time management skill.

Advertising-Marketing Manager: A specialized career niche in tour operation is that of handling the promotions and advertising for scheduled tour programs. Following up on emails, handling requests for information, and meeting with clients returning from a tour or cruise who may be planning a new trip are all part of this manager's day. The person placed in charge of advertising and promotions must stay current with new trends in E-commerce and other marketing opportunities.

Lead An Exciting Career as an International Tour Director

International tour directors lead and accompany passengers on multi-day tours. They manage arrangements and services and provide relevant information and commentary. Tour directors work for tour companies, resort chains, and transportation companies. The International Tour Director should have an outgoing personality, an interest in travel, geography, history and attractions, and good communication and presentation skills. Customer service skills and knowledge of the tour area are also necessary. Research skills, people and time management skills, and fluency in a second language are also desired. Their on the job responsibilities include:

- Provide general knowledge of attractions and destinations
- Develop and maintain an information file
- Prepare and deliver commentary
- Prepare for tour by making arrangements and confirming reservations
- Conduct tours
- Complete tour reports, daily logs and expense reports
- Assist special needs clients
- Escort passengers

Additional information: www.thegemgroup.org

Special Events, Conference and Convention Planner

Convention Planners create extravagant galas and regional expositions for trade shows and corporate meetings, and they organize and execute events and gatherings for public and business attendance.

Events and conferences contribute dollars to communities. Not only do travelers spend money on the event or conference itself, but also "spin-off dollars" are spent on everything from accommodations to souvenirs. Travelers need transportation to and from an event. Attendees need to eat, which affects the food and beverage sector. Conferences usually include social events and entertainment, so more dollars are spent on tickets, admission, beverages, and tips.

A growing number of special events encourage travelers to visit areas to which they may not otherwise go. Many of these events are so successful that they have become national or international attractions. Special events often include formal or informal meetings running in conjunction with the event, requiring space rentals, food and beverage purchases. and local transportation. The planning and organizing of special events can be complex and demanding. All facets must be precisely coordinated to ensure the event runs efficiently and profitably. Many paid positions are often available as well as volunteer opportunities to gain industry exposure and experience.

Business people frequently meet to share ideas and information, to solve problems or to develop new strategies or products, and/or to be trained. Organizations send their staff to sales meetings, professional development conferences, and networking conventions. Companies exhibit their wares at specialized exhibitions and trade shows. Club or association members, specialists in various fields, and special interest groups also gather at conventions. They travel across the country or across the globe. People meet as members of clubs, square dance associations, or Star Trek conventions.

The planning and organizing of any special event, conference or trade show can be complex and demanding. All facets need to be coordinated so that the event will run efficiently and profitably!

The Coordinator will hone existing skills or develop new ones to take on the role of the consummate party host and activities director, including:

- Conducting a full site survey
- Managing sponsorship branding of an event
- Assisting in sponsorship product deliveries
- Handling celebrity hospitality and transportation logistics
- Managing entertainment arrangements
- Conducting or supervising food preparation
- Ordering food from purveyors
- Handling shipping and receiving
- Doing food cost estimates
- Learning product timing (nothing should be cold unless it's supposed to be!)
- Learning beverage controls
- Purchasing wine & liquor
- Managing bar inventory systems
- Taking reservations including point-of-service (POS) systems and phones, day-to-day planning and seating, catering and special events
- Learning day-to-day receivables & payables
- Booking entertainment – bands, DJs, and promotional events
- Conducting public relations
- Learning how to build the right branding and marketing relationships
- Sitting in on an interview with possible job applicants to learn how to hire the right staff for service and kitchen
- Obtaining permits and licenses (what they need to open the door)

Special events coordinators assist in the preparation, implementation, execution, and evaluation of special events. They help with human resource coordination by recruiting, training, and motivating staff and volunteers. It is a job that requires creativity and the use of many talents. Event coordinator positions may be short-term contracts, and many event coordinators move from contract to contract and event to event.

On-the-Job Responsibilities: Administer financial controls and procedures; implement event plans, including program, site development, equipment, staging, seating, and parking; co-ordinate office administration; fulfill marketing plan including advertising, trade shows, contests and volunteer/sponsor appreciation programs; recruit train, supervise, and evaluate staff and volunteers; prepare/deliver written and verbal communications.

Special Note: Since conferences and special events are big business to communities, most cities and regions have convention and visitor bureaus, with marketing and sales departments that spend money and time (up to ten years to lure a new major convention) to attract tourism business to their area.

Employment Resources:
- International Association of Conference Centers: www.iacconline.com
- b-there.com: www.b-there.com
- Society of Corporate Meeting Professionals: www.scmp.org
- Tradeshow Week: www.TradeshowWeek.com

Travel-Tourism Resources:
- Institute of Certified Travel Agents: www.icta.com
- International Airlines Travel Agent (IATAN) www.iacanorg
- The Boyd School: www.boydschool.com
- National Tour Association: www.ntaonline.com
- U.S. Tour Operators Association (USTOA) www.ustoa.com
- www.thegemgroup.org "Start Your Own Travel-Tourism Business
- Association of Destination Management Executives: www.adme.org
- Tourism Offices Worldwide directory: www.towd.com
- International Association of Convention & Visitor Bureaus: www.iacvb.org

Discount & FREE Travel & Cruises! Better know as "FAM TOURS" for members of the travel-tourism industry, these educational site inspections are sponsored by airlines, tour operators, hotels and government tourism offices to acquaint reservation agents and the sales staff with what a cruise ship or destination has to offer. During the trip, the participants are kept occupied morning, noon, and night visiting sites, hotels, restaurants, and attractions. Through these "FAM" trips, the agents get first-hand knowledge about the destination/cruise line. In the evenings the agents attend a series of local performances, dinners, cocktail parties, and receptions.

"If you like to be outdoors and active… discover a career in outdoor adventure!"

Eco-tourism, adventure tourism, and recreation are growing fast, thanks to changing trends in travel and tourism. Driving this growth is the request by today's active clients for recreation and travel adventures where experiencing nature and culture are part of the plan.

Special Note: Over the past four decades, the nature of tourism has developed in scope and direction, away from traditional tourism, such as the "Three Ss" (sun, sand, sea) to a wide range of activities including adventure, heritage and cultural tourism, special events and sporting challenges.

Nature Guiding Careers

Nature guiding offers numerous courses and activities for the great outdoors! If you are physically fit and have a taste for adventure and the great outdoors, you can choose to offer guide services and lectures in a variety of fields:

- Bird watching
- Salmon fishing
- Horseback riding
- Whitewater rafting
- Golf
- Wilderness trekking
- Hiking
- Cycling

- Mountaineering
- Canoeing
- Kayaking
- Sailing
- Scuba diving
- Sky diving
- Snow-mobiling
- Nature/wildlife viewing

Where do the clients come from?

Adventure tourism and recreation draws those who want to experience the country as a place that is natural and unspoiled, and those seeking active, unusual vacations.

Duties of an Adventure, Recreational, and Instructor Tour Guide

Adventure tourism and recreation is growing fast. Changing trends in travel and tourism, where clients request active recreational experiences or travel adventures where they can learn about nature and/or culture, are driving the growth. This sector includes everything from bird watching to salmon fishing, horseback riding to white water rafting, golf to wilderness trekking. Adventure tourism and recreation draws those who want to experience a place that is natural and unspoiled, and those who want active, unusual vacations. Because activities often mean clients need transport, hotel rooms, and restaurants, other tourism sectors also benefit.

Outdoor Adventure Guides

Overview: Organize and conduct expeditions for sports enthusiasts, adventurers, tourists or resort guests. You may work for adventure tourism companies, resorts, parks, lodges or campgrounds, or operate your own small business. You might take clients white water rafting, fishing, hunting, or mountain climbing.

Duties & Responsibilities:

- Guide individuals or groups
- Create positive customer relations
- Assemble necessary equipment and supplies
- Set up and break camp
- Prepare and/or serve meals
- Instruct and demonstrate related skills and techniques
- Respect and maintain natural resources

Another popular summer sport is tennis. Many clubs and resorts offer tennis courts, tennis lessons, and tennis gear. This is also an important part of the industry, with revenue earned through the sale of clothing and gear, the rental of courts, the training of players and the maintenance of equipment.

Golf and tennis pros, those who fix equipment and maintain courts and greens, those who work in industries that support the golfers and tennis players - all work in this area of the adventure tourism and recreation sector.

Additional skills and on the job experience: Physical ability and experience in the relevant sport or activity are required. An ability to get along with and work well with others is necessary, too. Excellent communication and instruction skills are required, as are organizational and leadership skills. Knowledge of terrain, the environment, and the local area in which the guide is to travel are all-important. Customer relations skills and equipment maintenance and repair skills are desired for this position, as is knowledge of outdoors cooking. It is also essential to know relevant laws and safety and emergency procedures.

Outdoor adventure and eco-tourism businesses require staff who have a love and knowledge of the outdoors. They often need technical proficiency and expertise in the activity that the business focuses on. In addition, in order to ensure the long-term viability of the business, they must respect the environment and help others to respect it as well.

Advanced training opportunities for the adventure tour guide: For High adventure – skiing, mountain climbing, and other extreme adventures, the North American Tour Guides are now adopting the European standards. The International Federation of Mountain Guides Association (IFMGA) has set the European standard for guiding, the most highly regarded guiding certification in the world -- and you have to risk your life repeatedly to obtain this certification! For starters, it takes three to five years of in-the-field training before you're even considered for IFMGA exams. Furthermore, IFMGA certification requires mastery of rock climbing, alpine skiing, and ski mountaineering. Aspiring guides must lead IFMGA examiners through whiteouts, belay them into technical *couloirs*, and otherwise get them safely and efficiently up and down cliff-ridden and avalanche-prone slopes.

As an outdoor guide, your job is to safely take clients to places they can't get to by themselves, and to do this in a fun and educational way. A guide is a leader, but a good guide listens to his clients and observes their abilities. It's your responsibility to make clients want to return by providing a trip that resembles what the company advertises. You want the client to tell their friends, and you hope they give you a nice tip in appreciation of your good service. As a freelance guide, you need to maintain good relations with several companies, providing quality trips according to the company's standards.

Guides & Pro-Instructors for Ski Resorts

Over six million North Americans regularly ski or snowboard. There are hundreds of alpine ski areas in North America and hundreds of ski clubs to serve them. These resorts attract skiers and snowboarders from across the country and large numbers of foreign travelers from around the world, especially from Japan, Britain, and Germany. Ski-related jobs are numerous. They are available at ski resorts, hills and clubs, and in those businesses that support the industry, like lodges and ski shops.

Additional Job Opportunities:
- Property Management
- Director of Sales
- Ticket Sales Manager
- Special Events Manager
- Public Relations Director

- Guest Services Director
- Mountain Manager
- Ski Patrol
- Rental Manager
- Snowmaking Director

Fishing Lodge Guide & Instructor

Qualifications: A good tour guide is a "people person," good with oral and written communications, an entertainer, a problem solver with the ability to handle a crisis behind the scenes. The fishing guide should have knowledge of map reading and be meticulous in handling details of food preparation, first aid, and small engine repairs. Credibility is built on their decision-making skills. Physically, outdoor guides must have excellent stamina in order to work the long days required out fishing or guiding along brooks and river streams. Their typical day includes:

- Camp setup (early part of the season only), includes cooking, dining and shower/sauna tents
- Rising at 7am to review camp and make certain no critters have gotten into things during the night
- Cooking and hosting buffet breakfast, lunch, dinner
- Planning the day with the staff and guides
- Communicating with air operator via radio regarding any incoming or return flights
- Go fishing!
- Filet and vacuum pack the catches of the day
- Start the evening's campfire….and relax after a wonderful day's work!

River Rafting Tour Guide

During the season this job is considered a LOT of hard work and can be a bit scary at times! It's a tough business, weather can be difficult. Group trips can be a challenge and Tour Guides must love their work, want to share their passion, history and provide a healthy supply of fun!

Typical responsibilities:

- Book and schedule guests
- Create staff schedule
- Conduct facility management
- Rig and launch rafts
- Assist in customer safety orientation
- Assess risk management
- "Read" the whitewater
- Assist in guiding raft
- Conduct equipment logistics
- Make common repairs
- Review state & federal guide requirements
- Natural & cultural history overview
- Overview of business start-up plan
- Business plan review
- Review Gantt (task flow diagram) charts for dual utilization of equipment

Heritage – Cultural- Historian - Interpretive Guide Careers

Should your interest be history, heritage, and culture, there will always be a need for your skills as a Interpretive Tour Guide, helping others understand and appreciate cultural or natural heritage. They work in many different settings - from parks, museums and aquariums to industrial sites, interpretive centers and botanical gardens. Interpreters do not simply lecture -- they have a complete understanding of their subject matter and share their knowledge with others. Different audiences make this position interesting and stimulating.

On-The-Job-Responsibilities

- Develop and deliver educational or cultural programs
- Adapt to different learning styles and participant needs
- Operate presentation equipment (e.g. audiovisual, overheads, slide shows, etc.)
- Protect resources.

The interpretive tour guide should exhibit good communication and public speaking skills, as well as maintain a good attitude and have an interest in and knowledge of related natural or cultural heritage. Experience in research is also necessary, as is customer service experience. Interpretive experience may be requested, plus experience working with groups. Desired skills and experience include leadership and problem-solving skills, and knowledge of the area, its heritage, and tourism in general.

Employment & Resources

Institute of Certified Travel Agents: www.icta.com

International Airlines Travel Agent (IATAN) www.iacanorg

The Boyd School: www.boydschool.com

National Tour Association: www.ntaonline.com

U.S. Tour Operators Association (USTOA) www.ustoa.com

The GEM Group Ltd. www.thegemgroup.org

Museum Curator-Interpretive Guide Careers

Where you can work: Museums, theatres, galleries, heritage & historical sites, parks, gardens, interpretive centers, cultural tourism, industrial tourism, aboriginal tourism. General Manager Curators are specialists in a particular academic discipline relevant to a historic site/museum/gallery's collection. Museum Curators research and recommend acquisition of artifacts and are responsible for the care of objects, materials and specimens. They have highly specialized skills and knowledge in their areas of study.

An Interpretive Guide Skills: The guide should have excellent communication skills, especially when working as a Museum Curator, plus experience in a museum, gallery or related educational or research organization. A Curator also must have evidence of research and writing, and specialized knowledge in the area relevant to museum collections. Desired experience and skills include knowledge of other specialty areas, an ability to interpret collections and to communicate that knowledge. Also, knowledge of the ethics of collecting, the current market, as well as customs regulations is preferred. Many of these positions require a college degree in such fields as anthropology, history, or art history.

On-the-Job-Duties:

- Interpret materials or artifacts for the public and/or for other museum staff
- Recommend acquisitions, loans or sales research
- Authenticate history of artifacts
- Coordinate the storage of collections
- Use proper conversation methods
- Set up displays and exhibitions
- Supervise assistants

Career & Employment positions:

- Museum Guide
- Visitor Services Manager
- Ride Operator

- Concession Attendant
- Retail Shift Supervisor
- Interpretive Specialist
- Attractions Guide
- Retail Sales Clerk
- Maintenance/Grounds Supervisor
- Amusement Park Supervisor

Employment Opportunities & Travel-Tourism Resources:

- Association for Living History, Farm and Agricultural Museums
  www.alhfam.org/alhfam.jobs.html
- **International Association of Convention & Visitor Bureau** www.iacvb.org
- National Tour Association- www.ntaonline.com

For schools and additional training:

- www.mtnguide.net
- www.mountain-guiding.com
- www.alpineascents.com
- www.aai.cc
- www.thegemgroup.org

Convention Sales Manager

This manager opens new markets for meetings, conventions, and trade shows; develops leads and assists in closing group business on behalf of a local convention center; organizes the conventions and meetings that have been booked. The manager uses expertise in keeping costs to a minimum; makes recommendations for amenities, unique venues, local speakers, and themes; may be responsible for handling hotel and local touring and transportation.

Tourism Marketing Coordinator

This staff member coordinates the bureau's participation in domestic and international trade shows; helps arrange familiarization tours to the destination by media and the travel trade; and arranges seminars for travel press and members of the travel-tourism industry, and prospective clients.

Other opportunities working for state or local convention boards:

- Special Events Coordinator
- Market Research Analyst
- Director of Advertising
- Convention Sales Manager
- Market Research analyst
- Director of Public Relations
- Manager of Information Technology
- Director of Membership Services

Visitor Information Counselor

The Visitor Information Counselor is responsible for identifying tourism opportunities. States, cities and local communities draw visitors to destinations for stays of varying lengths and generates tourism revenue community-wide. Every country has major and minor attractions to lure visitors and generate tourism revenue. Many attractions are educational in nature, while others are solely for entertainment. From educational visits to entertaining stops, attractions facilities offer unique, memory-making experiences that include activities and venues that often form the beginning of travel plans.

Attractions and sites requiring entry level and management staff:

- historic sites
- heritage homes
- museums
- halls of fame
- art galleries
- botanical gardens
- aquariums, zoos
- water parks
- amusement parks
- casinos
- cultural attractions

Being a visitor information counselor plays an important part or "link" between the visitor and the State/City tour office. You are in the front lines, providing answer to questions about the area, history, attractions and weather. Much of the time is spent talking to the visitor. One should have excellent communication skills and good customer service skills. Knowledge of attractions, events and the local area is also required. Other useful abilities are research and recording skills, sales and cash handling, inventory and administrative skills. Knowledge of a second language can be helpful, especially when working in areas where travelers may not speak the local language.

On-The-Job Responsibilities:

- Answer questions and provide information specific to region or site
- Distribute promotional material
- Promote Tourism products
- Encourage new and return visits
- Gather information and develop new resources
- Perform administrative tasks
- Stock brochures, maps and sell merchandise and handle cash transactions

Other Career and Employment Opportunities:

- Director of Tourism
- Deputy Commissioner
- Sales and Marketing - Domestic
- Sales and Marketing - International
- Art, design manager
- Tour packaging
- Familiarization host
- Visitor Information Counselor

Working for the National and State Parks Service

The National Parks/State Parks job is to conserve natural scenery, protect wildlife and historic sites and objects, and provide for the public enjoyment of these areas -- and under the watchful eye of the park serve personnel, ensure the visitor leave the sites, trails and waterways unimpaired.

Employment and career and employment Opportunities National & State Parks

- Park Warden,
- Park Interpreter,
- Marina Attendant,

- Golf/Tennis Pro,
- Ski Lift Operator
- Golf Operations Manager,
- Public Relations Manager
- Sports Equipment Repair Person

The Parks supervisor and his/her assistant are responsible for:

- Development of historical features
- Guide interpretation
- Law enforcement and wildlife management
- Protection of the natural surroundings
- Daily administration of personnel duties and reports
- Assigning duties for park facilities maintenance

State/Regional Park Ranger "Smoky the Bear"

The Park Ranger's duties involve patrolling the waters, lakes, and streams, ensuring that d visitors follow all laws and regulations set forth by the National and State Parks system.

Additional duties include:

- Create programs for the parks
- Prepared to answer questions and manage information center
- Handle public relations
- Manage records and budgets
- Issue Park fishing and boating permits
- Control the visitor activities on paths, trails and roads
- Maintaining a ongoing count of visitors to avoid overcrowding space
- Check on camping and RV sites
- Monitor fishing, hunting limits
- Enforce "Fire Safety"

City Parks Recreation Programmer

As a city parks manager or assistant, you will be responsible for setting up programs and sporting events for youth, handicapped, and senior citizens. There will be occasions where you will set up educational activities. Planing daily and extended tour programs are also initiated at the City Parks level for youth and senior citizens. Additional programs include special events, art, crafts and games.

Employment Opportunities & Travel-Tourism Resources

Society of Government Travel Professionals www.government-travel.org

National Recreation and Park Association
2775 South Quincy Street
Suite 300
Arlington, VA 22206

U.S. Department of the Interior
National Park Service'1849 c Street, NW
Washington, DC 20240

Motor Coach-Rail-Cruise Lines-Airlines

Tourism was earlier defined as an industry that provides for the movement, comfort and enjoyment of people. The 'movement' in this definition is addressed by the transportation sector. Air, railway, water, and ground transport provided 267,600 positions in 1997 and is expected to generate 27,800 new jobs by 2006.

The sector is divided into four categories: Air, Rail, Ground, and Water.

Special Note: Escorted motor coach tours are growing! There is a need for tour planners, reservation agents, and sales and marketing pros, as well as tour escorts.

Employment opportunities in the Motor Coach Industry:

- Owner/Manager
- Tour Planner/Designer
- Reservation Agent
- Tour Director/Tour Escort
- Advertising Executive
- E-commerce programmer
- Web Designer
- Dispatching
- Mechanic
- Motor coach driver

Motor Coach Driver/Charter and Local Sightseeing Conductor

The motor coach charter business transports millions of visitors every day, providing tours in deluxe coached with air conditioning, restrooms, kitchens, bar services, videos, viewing decks. S a driver for a large tour company/charter operator, you will have the opportunity to travel to popular tourist spots. Bus drivers may work nights, weekends, and holidays. They often spend nights away from home, staying at hotels at company expense. The driver must have an excellent driving record and be able to offer information about the locale. Good health and physical fitness, tourism or customer service experience, and excellent communication skills are also necessary. A good driver must have organizational, record-keeping, destination knowledge, routes, and legislation and regulations skills. A second language is also an asset.

On-The-Job-Responsibilities:

- Make routine checks of coach
- Greet customers,
- Confirm destination, tour itinerary and wok with tour director/tour escort
- Assist passengers on and off coach
- Practice defensive driving
- Be prepared to provide tour commentary
- Offer information on locale, attractions, and restaurants
- Maintain trip and maintenance log

Charter Motor Coach - Tour Director

The work is 24/7 while on the road.. It is emotionally and physically demanding. A good escort must have patience and know how to deal with people. A good Tour Director/Tour Escort must display leadership's skills, be detail-oriented, well organized and highly responsible and be prepared to mange emergencies and large amounts of money.

On-The-Job-Responsibilities:

- Meet and Greet tour members
- Conduct tour
- Explain tour itinerary, stops along the way, restaurants
- Care for special need passengers
- Organize activities on and off the motor coach
- Provide information on locale, attractions
- Respond to emergencies, accidents or medical problems
- Maintain records on all expenditures
- Keep notes on hotels, attractions, food service, step-on-guide service with recommendations for their employer

Director of Sales and Marketing for Charter Motor Coach Companies

Sales and marketing directors are responsible for establishing and directing the marketing and sales activities of the company. They may co-op the marketing efforts with the attractions sector, such as zoos, museum, amusement parks, or heritage sites, hotels or resorts. Sales and marketing directors direct the activities of staff involved in sales, reservations, marketing, advertising and public relations; and in doing so, they impact the direction and goals of a the motor coach company. A good sales director should have experience in sales, marketing, public relations and/or the travel-tourism industry. Proof of previous sales success will be required. Leadership and teambuilding skills, good communications skills, human resource and financial management skills, and time management skills are also necessary. This position requires strategic planning and business skills and a strong network of contacts.

On-the-Job-Responsibilities:

- Assign sales territory, target groups and sales quotas
- Co-ordinate sales activities with other work units or departments
- Prepare and submit plans, budget, progress reports and annual sales reports
- Manage human resource functions, e.g. hiring, training, performance reviews

- Research competitors' products/tour programs
- Develop goals and objectives, projects and priorities, and assign them to sales manages and staff
- Develop and conduct sales campaigns and marketing and promotional plans

Additional job opportunities:

- Mechanic
- Tour Planner

Career Resources:

- Greyhound Lines, Inc: www.greyhound.com
- National Tour Association: www.ntaonline.com
- American Bus Association: www.buses.org
- National Motor coach Marketing Network: www.motorcoach.com
- International Association of Tour Managers (IATM): London, England   071-703-9154

Rail Service-Amtrak-North America

Amtrak & Via Rail, national passenger rail service carries approximately 8.3 million passengers annually. There are also smaller regional railways that employ staff for positions from selling tickets to operating the train. Rail travel is a relaxed, scenic way to travel, and is becoming increasingly popular as a vacation, rather than only as a way to get to a vacation spot.

Amtrak over the years has become innovative in attracting more passengers traveling for vacations and business. New offerings of equipment include the Metroliners, superliners, luxurious bi-level cars, sleepers, AmFleet cars, Heritage cars, Turboliners, Vista Dome coaches all encouraging an increase in rider ship. New jobs and emphasis in training and development is producing new career opportunities with Amtrak.

Rail Engineer

Their hands are on the "throttle," and they are responsible for passengers and freight. Being a rail engineer is a dream job for many who want to 'ride the rails." They must keep their eyes on the rails looking for obstructions, cars/trucks stuck on the rails, and be in constant contact with dispatchers and conductors.

Railroad Conductor

Railroad conductors supervise service attendants and, as well, participate in providing guest services to passengers on trains. They operate the public address system, updating travelers on approaching stops. They offer information, answer inquiries, communicate with the locomotive crew, and periodically check train systems and equipment. Being a railroad conductor requires travel of one day or extended trips. Customer service experience, supervisory or management experience, leadership qualities and team-building skills are all required for this position. Good judgment, problem-solving skills and strong communication skill are also necessary.

On-The-Job-Responsibilities:

- Manage human resources, supervising staff in completion of their duties
- Respond to customer inquiries and complaints
- Provide customer services, such as ensuring safety procedures are followed
- Supervise baggage and seating arrangements

Addition career and Employment Opportunities:

- Engineering
- Maintenance
- Dinning room service (bar tenders/chefs/wait staff)
- Station Personnel:
- Reservations
- Sales and Marketing
- Reservations-Ticket Agents

Career Information:

Amtrak National Railroad Passenger Corporation: www.amtrak.com

Cruise Lines Industry: "A Global Community"

In the 1970s, the television show, *The Love Boat,* gave Americans a glimpse of what cruising was like – and they began to realize that cruising was not a pastime for the super-rich but affordable for the average vacationer. They saw the possibility of visiting exotic locales, eating gourmet meals, and enjoying endless shipboard entertainment including shows, movies, dancing, lectures, games, gambling, health spas, and sports. Cruises are now carrying over 2,000 passengers offering many career opportunities

Jobs in the Cruise Industry

Traditionally cruise lines hired people from abroad for entry-level work. Times are changing, and more North Americans are being recruited from hotel schools or starting out in reservations.

It is important to remember that many ships are registered abroad and hire personnel from their home ports to staff them. With the increase of North Americans cruising the seven seas, opportunities such as purser, gift shop attendant, beautician, casino dealer, social director, medical staff, and information system manger are opening up for North Americans. Once you have reached mid-management positions, opportunities open up both on-shore and aboard the cruise ship.

Ships vary in size and are staffed with employees from around the world. Cruise lines will assign responsibilities to different departments and staff members, such as:

- Deck Department
- Engine Department
- Food and Beverage Department
- Hotel Department Purser's Department
- Cruise Department
- Service Department

- Passenger Service Representative (PSR)
- Port Lecturer
- Hostess
- Assistant Excursion Manager

Home Office employment opportunities: It is not necessary to work aboard a ship to be associated with the cruise line industry. It's possible to find work in administration, sales, marketing, finance, management information systems, and operations. The cruise lines are primarily located in Miami, Ft. Lauderdale, Port Canaveral, Los Angeles, Vancouver, New York, San Juan and San Diego, offering positions in such fields as:

- Reservations
- Controller and Accounting
- Sales and Marketing
- Sales promotions and other executive positions

You may opt for self-employment by starting your own "Cruise Only Agency" as an associate of the GEM Group Ltd. (www.thegemgroup.org)

Passenger Service Representative

Depending upon the assignment, you could be responsible for escorting clients to the cruise ship and while en route, providing a brief overview of their itinerary , visas, passports, or custom regulations pertaining to the embarking country. Most important – you must make sure no luggage gets lost!

Additional On-The-Job responsibilities aboard ship:
- Reconfirm all flight departures for the passengers return home
- Process disembarkation
- Oversee tagging off all passenger luggage and assist in airport transfers and check-in
- After seeing passengers off, the PSR is responsible in collecting passengers comments cards and discuss with management the grading and comments made by the guest regarding food service, shore excursions, entertainment and interest in ports of call.

Activities Director

The cruise line activities directors serve as hosts on cruise ships. They organize activities and ensure that passengers enjoy themselves. In this exciting position, recreation/activity directors are on call 24 hours a day while cruising. When they are away from home, they have opportunities to explore new destinations and see new sites. A professional attitude and appearance are required, as are special event/group activity planning skills and good communication and presentation skills. Tourism or customer service experience is an asset, as is knowledge of ships, navigation, destinations, and attractions. Also useful are organizational and record-keeping skills and time management skills. A second language can often be helpful.

On-the-Job responsibilities:

- Meet and greet passengers
- Conduct tours of ship, introducing passengers to the captain and crew
- Demonstrate and explain safety procedures
- Care for special-needs passengers
- Organize activities, such as sports, entertainment and tours
- Provide information on locale, attractions, fares, etc.
- Respond to emergencies, accidents or medical problems
- Keep records and logs

Employment Opportunities & Travel-tourism Resources:

- *How to Get a Job on a Cruise Ship,* Author-Don Kennedy, Career South Publications
- Cruise Lines International association (CLIA) www.crusising.org
- International Council of Cruise Lines www.iccl.org

Sector Five

Airline Career and Employment Opportunities

Airline transportation remains the primary mode of domestic travel after private vehicles. The 'Open Skies Agreement' reached in February 1995 allows airlines (instead of governments) to decide which trans-border routes they want to fly. Since then, trans-border traffic has increased by 31%. With increased traffic comes the benefit of more jobs in the industry.

As passenger traffic continues to increase, airports are undergoing major renovations, and are expanding retail operations and marketing efforts. This also means new positions are created. There were more than 65,000 people employed in air transport services in 1997.

Airline Pilot

Overview: Pilots are skilled individuals who fly or assist in the flight of the aircraft, either fixed-wing (airplanes) or rotary-wing (helicopters). They may fly passengers from one place to another on commercial flights, transport government or business personnel on private jets, or be employed to offer search and rescue services. Pilots may also be self-employed, and offer flights in and out of remote locations to hikers or hunters. This position is exciting and varied and requires steady, focused concentration and an ability to convert learning into skills at a moment's notice. Today most pilots have college degrees and have already had experience flying when they are hired by commercial airlines.

Duties: prepare flight plans, monitor weather conditions and plane requirements operate aircraft controls, communication and navigation systems direct activities of flight crew during flight monitor operation of engines and functioning of aircraft systems during flight are prepared to handle emergency situations.

Experience: Technical aptitude, good judgment and problem-solving skills, and strong communication skills are all required of a pilot. In addition, leadership qualities, the ability to work as a team member, and technological and navigational skills are necessary. Good health, hearing and vision, and height and weight that conform to safety standards are also essential. Desired experience and skills include time management skills, leadership and team building skills and emergency and disaster management skills.

Flight Attendant

The flight attendant's first priority is to make sure the passengers are safe, comfortable, and experience an enjoyable flight to their destination. Typically they will be home based in a major city or hub. Flight attendants are friendly, service-oriented professionals who work on planes and in airports. They are trained to help ensure the safety and comfort of passengers during airplane flights. They enjoy working as part of a team to ensure that customer service expectations are met. They are often away from home, and have an opportunity to see different parts of the world. Attendants must be well groomed, physically fit and in good health and must also conform to safety standards for height and weight. Good communication and interpersonal skills are required, as are excellent customer service skills. A second language may be a requirement, as a willingness to relocate and a willingness to attend approved airline training program. Experience in food and beverage service, knowledge of policies, procedures, and knowledge of tour-related geography and information, and time management skills are required.

Sample list of On-The Job-responsibilities:

- Prepare the cabin for the passengers arrival
- Check out the food and beverage supplies and carts
- Make sure all first aid kits and other emergency equipment is in working condition
- "Meet & Greet" the passengers and help them find their seats
- Prepare passengers for take off identifying exits and other emergency measures
- Check seat belts, store trays and store any loose luggage

While in flight:

- Serve passengers beverages and meals
- Distribute headphones for movies
- Sell duty-free items on some international flights
- Advise passengers how to fill out immigration, custom forms
- Prepare necessary forms and reports for their supervisors
- Advise passengers of connecting flights and their destination

Airline Reservationists

Qualified reservation and customer service agents are always in demand. They play an essential role in the airline industry by booking clients for flights. A reservationist must be a good typist with a sales background and be able to use the airline's computerized reservation system -- and be able to handle complaints when the weather turns bad and flights are cancelled.

Typical duties include:

- Receive and process reservations
- Book hotel and auto rentals and other travel reservations
- Maintain and record all reservations and confirmations
- Offer advice on destinations and destination activities
- Be trained on fare changes, schedules
- Collect payment for groups and individuals

Customer Service Representatives

New entry employees often start out working as ramp agents where baggage is sorted, marshalling the plane in with wands, and connecting power service to planes that have landed. The next career step is generally that of a customer service representative.

On-The-Job Responsibilities:

- Reissuing airline tickets

- Upgrading clients to first class based on frequent flyer points

- Handling seat assignments

- Becoming familiar with the departure gate operations

- Assisting in lost and found luggage

- Becoming trained in national and FAA security operations and procedures

Travel-Tourism Resources:

- Aviation Employee Placement Service: www.aeps.com

- College of Aeronautics, La Guardia Airport: www.aero.edu

- Aviation Information Resources: www.jet-jobs.com

- Airline Pilots Association, International: www.alpa.gov

Sector Six

Theme Parks-Attraction Centers and Broadway

Regardless of size, attractions venues need people to sell food and souvenirs, promote the attraction, maintain the facility, and manage the operation. This sector offers a wide variety of employment opportunities, ranging from seasonal part-time to permanent full-time positions.

> ***Special Note:*** Education and a degree in art can lead to positions as filmmakers, set builders and designers, production designers, and audio/video systems designers.

In the entertainment arena, tourist attractions on Broadway include Radio City Music Hall, the Metropolitan Museum or Art, and Lincoln Center. Theater goers come from around the world, and when productions take to the "road," they hire the services of travel professionals from all seven sectors of the travel-tourism industry.

Employment opportunities:

- International Sales Manger/Director
- Financial Planner
- Training and Recruitment Manager
- Public Relations
- Computer and graphics artists and designer

Attractions Ride Operator

Ride operators are charged with the safe operation of rides at amusements parks, fairs and festivals. As a ride operator, one must be constantly alert in order to monitor both the ride's operation and patrons' behaviors. Ride operators also maintain the upbeat, fun environment of the attraction, which adds to the enjoyment of the participants.

A ride operator must have good communication skills and be tactful and diplomatic. It is also desirable for the operator to have mechanical ability, customer service experience, knowledge of general safety procedures, and knowledge of the attractions and local area.

On-the-Job-Responsibilities:

- Perform routine maintenance and safety inspections on rides

- Maintain a clean and safe space in and around rides

- Collect tickets and operate ride

- Ensure the safety and enjoyment of all ride passengers

- Offer on-board narration when necessary

Special Employment Opportunities: Many attractions offer exciting opportunities that include acting, food service, management, and major chances for a rewarding career. Colonial Williamsburg (804.220.7129) is open 24 hours daily. Walt Disney Corporation (www.disneycareers.com) operates Disney World, Epcot, Disneyland, EuroDisney, and other attractions. Universal Studios in Hollywood and Orlando, Busch Gardens, Six Flags, and Dollywood (in Pigeon Forge, Tennessee) all need employees in may fields.

Travel-Tourism Resources:

- International Association of Amusements Parks and Attractions: www.iaapa.org

- www.alhfam.org/alhfam.jobs.htmal

- Association for Living History, Farms and Museums
  www.alhfam.orgalhfam.jobs.html

Sector Seven

Alternative Paths to Your Dream Job

Not all jobs in the travel-tourism industry fit neatly into traditional categories of providing or arranging guest services. You can be independent and pursue your dream in your own way instead of working for a travel bureau or airline or agency.

Travel Writer-Photographer

Travel writers and photographers travel the world to develop stories and take photos for travel-tourism sites. They are often contracted or employed by the travel-tourism industry newspapers and magazines, tourism boards and other government agencies. Experience as a travel writer requires creative ability as well as the technical skill to take photographs. Physical stamina for travel and interviewing skill to create stories is valuable to a travel writer-photographer.

On-the-Job responsibilities:

- Research subject
- Travel to and explore destinations
- Conduct interviews
- Write and edit articles prior to editorial review (writer only)
- Take photographs, identify/gain consent of subject (photographer only)
- Develop and enhance photographs (photographer only)
- Deliver work, often by electronic means

Employment Opportunities & Travel-tourism Resources:

- Society of American Travel Writers www.satw.org
- Travelwriters.com www.travelwriters.com
- PhotoSecrets Travel Photography www.photosecrets.com/links.html
- Inkspot (Travel Writers Spot) www.inkspot.com/genres/travel/markets.html

Teacher-Trainer for the Hospitality-Tourism Industry

The demand for good educators with a strong background in the travel-tourism industry has grown tremendously due to the explosion in enrollment and the dynamics of the industry. Educators teach hospitality and tourism at community colleges and universities. Instructors conduct classes and workshops for students. A strong background and work experience in the travel-tourism industry is necessary.

Overall Job Requirements:

- Skills in customer relationship service
- Communication
- Business management
- Sales and marketing
- Hotels background
- For teaching, appropriate degrees and credentials
- Familiar with major cruise lines and the transportation companies

Aside from education and training newcomers to the industry, many companies have their own in-house programs to raise productivity or advance workers to management level. Responsibilities for these instructors include preparing students for employment opportunities within the travel-tourism industry. Opportunities for employment as a qualified instructor will continue to expand as the travel-industry grows.

Travel-Tourism Resources:

International Society of Travel Tourism Educators www.istte.org

Travel and Tourism Research Association www.ttra.com

Travel-Tourism educators use their expertise to increase the professionalism and skills of those working in the travel-tourism industry. They work in training classrooms, work sites and in schools and have a good understanding of the travel-tourism industry as well as knowledge of adult learning principles and of training techniques. They may work as contract trainers, or may be employed by a company to manage ongoing training needs.

A travel-tourism education includes knowledge of adult learning principles and excellent interpersonal skills. Training or teaching experience is desirable.

On-the-Job Responsibilities:

- Plan training objectives and session plans
- Deliver training sessions
- Respond to questions and comments
- Develop and administer evaluations
- May develop program, curriculum or learning activities

Yacht Crew – River Boats

You can apply for positions with Windjammer Barefoot Cruises, Private World Yacht Enterprises; exploration ships that travel to Alaska and the Galapagos Islands via Lindblad Expeditions, and World Explore Cruises. For riverboat companies the Delta Queen operates out of New Orleans, Louisiana. Positions include:

- Chef/Cook
- Diesel Mechanic
- Flotilla Skipper
- Host & Hostess
- Sailing Instructor

Cruise line Resources:

- American Classic Voyages Company: www.amcv.com
- International Council of Cruise Lines: www.iccl.org

Ski & Spa Industry

The spa and ski industry affords an unparalleled opportunity to combine lifestyle with work. Both are specialized facets of the resort industry and present additional career paths for hospitality professionals. Both also draw on professionals from sports, health, and education. Whereas the ski industry is geographically more constricted (basically, anywhere there are mountains), the spa industry is much more widespread, and in many cases, is also an incorporated element of ski resorts.

Career Opportunities at Resorts and Spas

Resort and spa workers help guests at spas, luxury hotels, casinos, theme parks, and lodges. You may start out as a retail clerk or housekeeper and work your way up to a highly specialized game attendant or ski instructor.

Club Med and Sandals are the largest "all-inclusive" resorts s in the world for employment and training opportunities.

> *Hot Career Tip:* You can't beat working at resorts and spas for feeling as if you are on vacation year round!

Choosing the Ski Industry as a Career

The ski industry draws people who are committed -- even fanatical! -- about skiing and the outdoors. You get to ski, live and work amid incredible scenery, in the outdoors in pure air, working with people who tend to be active, outgoing, and energetic, while delivering a service that make people happy.

Career & Employment Opportunities:

- Marketing
- Group Sales
- Advertising and Public Relations
- General Manager-Resort
- Food & Beverage Service

- Ski School
- Ski Patrol
- Guest Services
- Mountain Manager
- Director of Lift Maintenance
- Maintenance Division

Travel-tourism Resources
- American Skiing Company www.peaks.com
- Cool Works: www. cool works.com
- Colorado ski Country, USA www. Colorado ski.com
- National Ski Areas Association www.nsaa.org
- Ski Tops-www.skitops.com
- Aspen Skiing Company www. skiaspen.com
- K&M Rocky Mountain Tours www.skithewest.com

Choosing the Spa Industry as a Career

Much like ski resorts, spa resorts have emerged as a subset of the travel industry and afford an opportunity to combine lifestyle (a devotion to health, fitness and wellness) with work.

"New Age" Retreats Careers

Spa resorts are expanding their markets from the staple of women seeking beauty or weight-loss treatments. Many are cultivating programs for men, and positioning themselves as places to find stress reduction and rejuvenation. They are cultivating new marketing initiatives, such as programs geared to bridal parties and incentives, which translate into jobs in marketing and sales. Becoming a Yoga/Nia Instructor at a New Age Retreat or at one of the famous international spas around the word offers expanding employment opportunities. Both women and men are seeking weight-loss treatments; beauty programs and stress reduction and rejuvenation. Having the proper training and certification puts you on the leading edge of the expanding spa industry.

Career & Employment positions:

- Administrative Assistant
- Aerobic Instructor
- Chef/Cook
- Boutique Staff
- Children's Program Coordinator
- Club Manager
- Dance Instructor
- Expedition Leader
- Hotel Manager
- Musician
- Overseas Representative
- Resort Administrator

Employment Opportunities in the Spa Industry:

Spafinders: www.spafinders.com

Spa-Therapy.com: www.spa-therapy.com

Spa Therapy: www.spa-therapy.com offer online specialist courses as well as jobs

An excellent source of locating spa resorts is www.spafinders.com

---

Want Something Completely Different in Your Career? Try www.funkycareers.com. This is an excellent website to search out unique employment opportunities worldwide.

Become a Private Pilot or Start Your Own Business

There are over 213,000 civilian aircraft and flight engineers employed in the United States of America. Commercial pilots who fly for the major airlines are among the highest paid workers in the country. The flight crew normally includes the captain, copilot, and flight engineer. Aside from flying with the major commercial lines, you can apply for positions as:

- Business pilot
- Flight instructor

- Photogrammetry pilot
- Facilities-flight-check pilot

Casino Employment Opportunities

Work in an industry that promotes gambling as a form of travel and recreation in international and domestic venues as riverboats, Native American Reservations, Trump Palaces and Casinos, racetrack and state lotteries. These workers help keep the operations running smoothly. Casino dealers conduct games in casinos and casino hotels. They deal cards and may handle large amounts of money. Mathematical skills and manual dexterity are required abilities for this position. A dealer must have a professional attitude and enjoy working with people. Cash handling experience is also necessary. Knowledge of the games is desired by employers, as are communication and customer service skills. You may work evenings, weekends and holidays and late into the morning.

Employment Opportunities: Casinos, a rapidly growing segment of the attractions sector, adds many new positions, such as pit bosses and dealers, to the labor pool.

- Games
- Security
- Hotel
- Food & Beverage
- Finance
- Slots
- Marketing
- Facilities
- Surveillance

The travel-tourism industry has experience a new wave of career opportunities related to technology and the rise of the worldwide web. Selling tours, cruises, airline seats, and other travel related services on line is big business. Virtually every supplier and travel company is affected with a vast proportion already having their own presence on the Web. E-commerce has become the most dynamic aspect of travel, with each day offering new challenges such as shifting strategies, technologies and new travelers.

How does a travel supplier convert "lookers" into "bookers" overcoming these obstacles?

- Reducing the time of booking
- Filling out the necessary reservation forms
- Offering last minute "discounts"
- Easing access to the tours and cruises
- Responding to questions relating to their travel requests

With a background in online community programming, knowledge of the travel industry, and familiarity with HTML, chat and board software and strong client relationship skills you will be able to source the greatest of new jobs within the Travel-Tourism industry by operating an on-line travel business.

Sample responsibilities:

- *Point of Service Sales:* Duties include the management and development of POS/pre-tour travel quality control software.
- *Trip-Planning systems*: Allow client to review itineraries, respond to reservations
- *End-to-end travel management systems:* Developing automated booking systems, reporting , and travel and expense management
- *Global travel-management reporting software:* Collect global travel data from different locations around the world.

Additional E- Commerce Career and Employment opportunities:

- Quality control Coordinators
- Computer Specialists
- Trainers
- Web Developers
- Brand marketers
- Yield Management Experts
- Researchers
- Director of global agency solutions
- E-business technology marketing
- Director of information services
- Director of Strategic planning, marketing and sales

Hot Career Tip: Search travel web sites to find excellent leads for employment and career opportunities using on-line technology.

What Attracts You to the Travel Industry?

Earlier in this book you were asked whether you have the traits needed for success. If you have read this far, by this time you have concluded that you can make travel-tourism a career in the many areas available. Before going further, take a moment to think over the positives and negatives that these careers offer.

Positive Values of a Tourism Career

- ☑ Travel, free and discounted
- ☑ Fast Promotions
- ☑ Discount Travel
- ☑ Growing Industry
- ☑ Rapid increase in earnings
- ☑ Exciting
- ☑ Meeting new people

☑ On-going training

☑ Responsibility

☑ Full-Part time employment

☑ No lay-offs (unless you are a seasonal worker)

Negatives to Consider

☑ Long Hours

☑ Working on week-ends, holidays

☑ Stress

☑ Entry level-low pay

☑ No routine

☑ Frayed nerves

☑ Away from home

☑ Jet lag

☑ Lack of sleep

☑ Rude clients

☑ Repetition

Essential Skills to Advance your Career

☑ Computer Skills

☑ Physical Strength

☑ Foreign Languages

☑ Management skills

☑ People skills

☑ Detail oriented

☑ Be able to resolve problems

☑ **Remain calm in a crisis**

☑ Perform CPR under stress

☑ Well groomed

☑ Attitude of friendliness

☑ Education: College degree, certification, associate degrees

Chapter 4

Owning Your Own Travel-Tourism Business

Are You An Entrepreneur at Heart?

"Every sector of the travel-tourism business is supported by small business owners".

There are many benefits of being an entrepreneur and business owner in travel-tourism – not the least of which is having your career on your own terms. You call the shots. You decide how hard you want to work and whether you want to operate a small business or a large one. Owning a business is not for everyone. There are risks, but there is a sense of adventure, too. And you can enjoy the thrill of seeing your creation become a success.

An entrepreneur in the travel-tourism industry is defined as "a person who undertakes an enterprise or business, with the chance of profit or loss" - there are several interesting concepts in this definition that bear close examination.

First, a single person (although in some cases it can be a small group of people) encompasses the idea of individual responsibility for the success or failure of the enterprise. Leading a business requires a special set of skills and the willingness to take total responsibility for the outcome of the decisions made.

Second, starting something new, or taking over something that is new for the entrepreneur requires drive and initiative.

Third, the definition mentions "chance." An entrepreneur is going to risk something -- money, time, and reputation. This enterprise is not 100% guaranteed to work. And there is the potential for either profit or loss. As many entrepreneurs know, it is perfectly possible that a business or enterprise may fail as well as succeed. However, these elements of uncertainty are exactly what put an entrepreneur in a different category from many other people. The entrepreneur is a person who is willing to fail or succeed, expects risk, but also expects that the rewards, if they happen, will be great, and compensate for any risks undertaken. There are ways of reducing risks and maximizing rewards, mainly based on obtaining and using crucial information -- one major reason that education plays a vital role for today's entrepreneur.

Life Changes

Owning a travel-tourism business can change your life. Suddenly, instead of being able to simply do your job, you need to have knowledge of everything that happens in the whole business. You have to be aware of what is going right and what is going wrong, before it happens. Ultimately the responsibility is yours -- the buck stops here. So what would make anyone want to take on this kind of responsibility? Well, many people don't wish to own their own business exactly because of the responsibility. But for those who do, the rewards can be really good. Not only do you profit from the financial gains of a successful business but also you gain a reputation as a good businessperson, of being capable of running a successful organization, and of being able to put plans into action. With full responsibility comes full authority. If you own a business, you have the authority to be able to do what you want to do. Of course, you will probably ask for opinions and advice, particularly if you employ good and competent people, but the decisions will be yours, and you will have the credit for them. This means that you have to have the ability to make good decisions; for many people the basis of good decisions is a good education, allowing you to acquire the skills and knowledge you need to run and own a successful business.

Assuming the Role of Self-Employed-Owner/Manager

Before starting out, take some time and conduct a personal evaluation. Be prepared to evaluate your business strengths and weaknesses.

Entrepreneurs who run and manage their own business will require some, if not all, of these essential management skills:

- Background and experience in tourism
- Being able to define goals and objectives
- Identify realistic goals and objectives
- Give attention to detail and customer care – vital for success!
- Identify new ideas and be prepared to take action
- Organizational skills
- Leadership skills
- Financial management skills
- Knowing how to run an office
- Marketing, sales
- Conduct a market analysis
- Communication Skills
- Customer service.
- Be able to meet and exceed the visitors' expectations

First Business Essential: Prepare a Comprehensive Plan

Once the business choice has been established, obtain help in preparing a comprehensive written plan. Your comprehensive business plan needs to include:

- Long term objectives
- Description of your travel-tourism business
- Personnel you plan to hire
- Identification of funding needs to start your business, plus a completed application for a loan or investment including your financial data.

When can you expect to start making money?

The financial section should list startup costs, a balance sheet, income statement projections (for at least 3 years) and a break-even analysis. It also should include an action timetable.

Prepare a "To-Do" List In Your Startup Planning Stage

- Decide on legal business (i.e., sole proprietorship or a corporation)
- Research thoroughly your potential customer base
- Secure necessary capital
- Secure necessary permits, licenses
- Obtain need facilities, equipment
- Recruit and hire personnel
- Establish a comprehensive training program
- Hours of operation

Seven Profitable Business Opportunities

The travel industry has spawned new business opportunities in many Travel-Tourism sectors. Most business opportunities with tourism tend to come in the form of direct service jobs in tourist-related facilities and attractions:

Transportation

- Taxi
- Limo
- Boating
- Snowmobiles
- Sailing
- Horse and buggy rides

Lodging

- Hotels
- Bed &Breakfast Inns
- Campgrounds
- RV Parks
- Cabins

Dining/Entertainment

- Sit down restaurants
- Take-out restaurants

Retail gifts/Shopping

- Gift Stores
- Money Exchange
- Booking agencies for tours and other local excursions
- Film development and service
- Bar & Restaurant
- Arts & Crafts
- Local foods, herbs and spices
- Small winery or local drinks
- Drug Store
- Food & Beverages
- Web Cafes

Ground Services Touring

- Fishing Guide
- Historical, cultural guide
- Adventure Guide
- Golf Guide

Domestic and International Tour Directors

- Escorting groups around the world

The travel-tourism industry has shown over the years that it has the ability to generate new business opportunities when the rest of the economy is in a slump. For that reason alone, travel-tourism is now considered the nation's third-largest retail sales industry and the second-largest private employer. (*Source: TIA Foundation*)

It is no wonder that travel is now the biggest consumer category on the World Wide Web. Globalization has changed the orientation of companies in response to falling barriers and borders and open to new career/business opportunities

You can even work from home. The travel-tourism industry is very entrepreneurial. Starting out working from home as an independent contractor for a major tour company, cruise line offers the entrepreneur the choice of working full- or part-time. By becoming a member of the NACTA-National Association of Commissioned Travel Agents, you will receive information on many opportunities:

- Training programs
- Tour Operators/Cruise Lines looking for representation
- Sample contracts between suppliers and the independent contractor
- FAM tours for International tours and Cruises

Owning a Boat Charter Company or Being a River Boat Captain
(for small boats carrying 6-40 passengers)

This is an exciting entrepreneurial opportunity for someone with the knowledge of rivers and lakes and the skill to handle fishing and whitewater charters. Among the skills needed are:

- Education in river/lake piloting skills
- handling (wind, current)
- Docking the riverboat
- "Reading the river" -- watching for sandbars, snags, obstructions
- Learning deckhand skills
- Assisting as tour guide and junior Captain during cruises
- Locking through a lock and dam
- Reviewing river transportation, from canoes to barges

- Assisting in general riverboat maintenance

- Learning about riverboat traditions, history, lingo and terminology

- Education in river bird & vegetation identification, ecology and geology

- Riverboat stories and storytelling!

- Ability to handle boats and do small engine repair is a must

Visitor Accommodations ~ Providing a Place to Sleep

Accommodation is one of the largest and fastest growing sectors in the tourism industry. Accommodation services have experienced growth of 49% in the past few years. Reasons for this include a demand for travel extending beyond traditional seasons, such as conferences during the summer held at ski resorts; the growth of large hotel chains and increased interest in vacation or time-share housing; and increased interest in North America as a destination and the value of the US currency as a destination.

Types of Accommodation Businesses

Owners/operators for hotels, country inns, bed and breakfast inns, or farms must have experience in tourism to be successful. Providing these types of accommodations offers the opportunity to work flexible hours and meet new people. Organizational skills, marketing, sales, customer service skills, and good communication skills are also necessary. Financial management skills and office or business experience are assets, as is the ability to speak a second language.

Because destinations are promoting four-season tourism and extending beyond traditional season, (e.g. incentive trips, conventions, training workshops) new opportunities are being created. As a small business owner you can choose the type of accommodation you want to operate.

Hotels

Hotel properties usually cater to both business and pleasure travelers and offer a wide range of accommodation types:

- *Deluxe, airport and convention hotels* are generally located in urban centers or near airports. They are often large (over 150 rooms) and have a wide range of facilities and services (e.g. convention rooms, restaurants, shops, fitness centers). Many are members of a chain, meaning that the property is part of a larger company and has sister properties in other areas. For an individual employee, the benefit of working at a chain might be the ability to transfer to other properties in the chain.

- *All-suite hotels* are increasingly popular. Each unit contains the same facilities as an apartment, meaning the travelers has a private place for meetings (i.e. the dining room table) and a kitchen for cooking meals.

- *Smaller, privately owned hotels* offer lodging and many also contain a café or restaurant, and a beverage room.

- *Resort hotels and lodges* are usually located at or near recreational sites. Many offer guests a wide range of activities, such as golf, skiing, and tennis, riding or water sports. They may also offer entertainment (e.g. nightclubs, shops, piano bars, casinos, dinner theatre) and have convention facilities.

- *Motels, motor hotels and inns* are usually smaller (less than 150 rooms), less expensive facilities which appeal to overnight or short-stay travelers. Some motels are franchise or chain operations; others are independently owned and operated. Motels are often found in smaller communities, the suburbs of cities, and along major highways.

Bed and Breakfasts and Farm/Ranch Vacation Sites

These cater to people wanting a personal touch, a unique heritage or lifestyle setting, or a home-like atmosphere. Few accommodate more than 8 to 10 people. Prices and amenities vary greatly from operation to operation. There may not be many positions at these sites because many are owner-operated and small enough so that just one or two people can manage. However, a position at one of these sites can be as varied as any in the industry. At a farm or ranch, helping the guests saddle up in the morning might be part of the 'front desk' position!

Cabins, Cottages and Houseboats

Often located in recreation areas and offering facilities such as a beach, fishing rentals, playgrounds, these are often destination sites for travelers. Generally, stays are longer than a night or two and involve the whole family, including the dog.

Campgrounds

Campground Operators manage all aspects of private or public campgrounds in a safe and professional manner. The duties of a Campground Operator are diverse, requiring both people and mechanical skills. Some of the work is outdoors and seasonal. Campgrounds cater to travelers who have their own roof, usually a tent or motor home, but require a serviced site for it.

Campgrounds range in the services they supply, from wilderness sites with no services (except maybe an outhouse) to full power and water hookups, with complete restaurant, laundry, entertainment and washroom facilities. This type of accommodation generally appeals to travelers who want an inexpensive outdoor experience and/or related activities, such as hiking, canoeing, fishing, hunting or boating.

Youth Hostels

These are usually non-profit facilities catering to budget-conscious or adventure travelers. Guests supply their own sleeping bags, cook their own meals, and often sleep in dormitory-style rooms.

Operating Duties for All Accommodations

- Meet guests' needs related to overnight stays and meals
- Respond to inquires and solve problems
- Offer tourism information and promote local area
- Use business management, sales and marketing skills
- Complete financial management tasks
- Use administrative skills
- Maintain facility, equipment and supplies

Catering to Travelers Who Want to Shop

Retail businesses that benefit from tourism revenue are also part of the tourism services sector. The World Tourism Organization defines tourism simply as the activities of those who travel outside their usual environments. This broad definition means that many businesses benefit from tourism dollars every day. Gift shops and other retail business gain significant income from tourism revenue. Travelers who shop for items forgotten at home, souvenirs, telephone cards, or spa treatments while traveling contribute dollars to the local economy. Any businesses that are retail in nature are part of the tourism services sector.

Visitors Need To Be Fed! ~ Restaurant Operations

One out of every four retail establishments is an eating and drinking location. Food and beverage outlets can range from restaurants and bars to nightclubs and posh dining. There are two types of restaurants: traditional sit-down dining with table service; and take-out or "fast food" chains.

With ever-changing consumer preferences and increased competition, the food and beverage industry has become increasingly sophisticated in the way it handles management and corporate strategies. Many restaurants, especially chains, are diversifying, coming out with their own retail product lines. Specialty cafés market their products to airlines and offices. Food and beverage chains have found a niche in bookstores, department stores, and casinos. As the lines between traditional food and beverage operations and other industries blur, employers and employees alike will have to continue to react to changing customer expectations with innovative ideas and responses.

Starting Your Own Tour Guiding Company

Early travelers were often accompanied by guides who had become familiar with the routes from having made earlier trips themselves. When leisure travel became more commonplace in the 19th century, women and young children were not expected to travel alone, so relatives or house servants often acted as companions. Today, tour guides act as escorts for people visiting foreign countries and provide them with additional information on interesting facets of life in another part of the world. In a way, tour guides have taken the place of the early scouts, acting as experts in the setting and in the situations tourists find unfamiliar.

Providing a Tour Guide Service

Guide services can encompass many tours to many types of locations, such as cultural sites, historic sites, and wine-tasting tours.

What It Takes to Be a Tour Guide

- Physical stamina and fitness
- In-depth knowledge on the subject area
- An ability to get along and work well with others
- Excellent communication and instruction skills
- Organizational and leadership skills
- Knowledge of local museums, national parks and local traditions and arts and crafts Customer relations skills
- Developing a network of support services, such as restaurants (rest stops), hotels and transportation companies

Starting out. Guiding tours for an established tour company is a good introductory position. Tour guides' lives are very busy when the peak season for tours arrives. Due to weather and traditional calendars for schools, most families with school age children tend to use the months of May through early September for excursions. When tour guides have a group to escort, their main goal is for every customer to be happy with the trip.

> ***New Vacation Trends:*** Some schools are now holding classes year round, so the time children are free for travel can be in almost any season instead of the summer months. In addition, empty-nester couples and retirees are finding the fall and spring ideal for travel to avoid the heavy crowds in the summer. There is a growing market for seniors tours, providing low-cost tour opportunities in off-peak vacation months.

New Business Opportunities

During the past century, the nature of tourism has developed in scope and direction, away from traditional tourism, such as the "Three Ss" -- sun, sand, sea -- to a wide range of activities including adventure, heritage, and cultural tourism, special events and sporting challenges.

Heritage Interpreters

These guides help others understand and appreciate cultural or natural heritage. They work in many different settings -- from parks, museums, and aquariums to industrial sites, interpretive centers and botanical gardens. Interpreters do not simply lecture; they have a complete understanding of their subject matter and share their interests and knowledge with others. The different audiences make this position interesting and stimulating.

Typical Duties:

- Develop and deliver educational or cultural programs
- Adapt to different learning styles and participant needs
- Operate presentation equipment (e.g. audiovisual, overheads, slide shows, etc.)
- Protect resources

Experience: Good communication and public speaking skills, as well as a good attitude and an interest in and knowledge of related natural or cultural heritage are all required of a Heritage Interpreter. Experience in research is also necessary as is customer service experience. Interpretive experience may be requested, as might experience working with groups. Desired skills and experience include leadership and problem-solving skills, and as well, a knowledge of the area, its heritage and of tourism in general.

Tour Guide -Adventure Tours

Adventure, Heritage, and Outdoor tourism and recreation are growing fast thanks to changing trends in travel and tourism. Driving the growth is the request of today's active clients for recreation and travel adventures where experiencing nature and culture are part of the plan.

Outdoor Adventure Guide

These guides organize and conduct expeditions for sports enthusiasts, adventurers, tourists or resort guests. They work for adventure tourism companies, resorts, parks, lodges or campgrounds, or they operate their own small businesses. They might take clients white water rafting, fishing, hunting, or mountain climbing, depending on the season and on their skills. Often the work is seasonal, and, depending on the type of guiding, the hours can be irregular.

Duties include:

- Guiding individuals or groups
- Creating positive customer relations
- Assembling necessary equipment and supplies
- Setting up and breaking camp
- Preparing and/or serving meals
- Instructing and demonstrating related skills and techniques
- Respecting and maintaining natural resources

- Local wineries
- Culinary "Dine a- rounds" and cooking classes
- Nature hikes
- Fishing-Hunting
- Kayaking
- Ghost Walks
- History Tours
- Pub tours
- Family reunions
- Weddings
- Learner's Quest Tours
- Treasure Hunts
- Artist Workshops
- Christmas & New Years celebrations
- Black History
- Religious tours
- Gay & Lesbians tour and events

Tour Guiding Services for Cruise Lines

Offer your services to visiting cruise ships within your region or become a member of the cruise lines and tour passengers at different ports of call. This is a great opportunity for independent tour guides who like the freedom of working on a contract basis.

***For additional information on starting a Tour Guide Company*:**

Contact www.thegemgroup.org or the GEM Consulting Service-1-800-894-TOUR.

Starting an In-Bound Destination Management Company

Opening an In-Bound Destination Tour Management firm provides you with the opportunity to offer four-season tours. There are many emerging specialty niche tours that In-Bound Destination Tour Managers can provide:

- Eco-tourism
- Soft & High adventure
- Hiking
- Horse Back Riding
- Shopping Tours
- Museum and other cultural venues
- Fishing
- "Hub-Spoke" itineraries where clients remain at one location and take daily trips to other areas of the region.
- Special events, conventions and special interest groups

The In-Bound Destination Management firm will be required to provide multilingual guides and have knowledge of the region and hotel accommodations. There will be opportunities to service incoming tour operators from abroad or other part of North America. Requests for your services will also include assistance and representation for local conventions, meetings, and corporate, professional, and academic groups and individuals as well as their spouses (and their children) by organizing supervised activities when parents are attending convention functions.

Operating an In-Bound Destination Management firm is a highly entrepreneurial field. Consider what your region has and doesn't have to offer. Become a member of the local tourism bureau and the Chamber of Commerce. Hosting incoming visitors is an exciting way to show civic pride and be creative.

Hot Job Tip: Love the outdoors? Conduct expeditions for sports enthusiasts, high- and soft-adventure tours, fishing, hunting, trekking, whitewater rafting. Often the work is seasonal, and depending on the type of guiding done, the hours can be irregular.

Designing and Escorting Tours for the Physically Challenged

This is a fast-growing industry! In North America alone, there are over 54 million people with various physical disabilities who have a desire to travel either by coach or cruise lines. "Disability does not mean inability!" To learn more about possibilities of becoming a tour guide/tour operator for the disabled, contact the Society for Accessible Travel & Hospitality (SATH) at www.sath.org.

To provide other services you should contact some of the major tour companies specializing in travel for those with disabilities. These include:

- Fly Wheels Travel Service   www.flyingwheelstravel.com
- Wilderness Inquiry 612-379-3858
- TKTS-N-Tours Travel www.ticketsntours.com
- Travel Aides International http://www.members.tripod.com

Should you or anyone you know have training in physical therapy or nursing, this travel specialty niche offers an excellent opportunity of get involved in serving the disabled and enjoy a tourism career at the same time.

Other Tour Guide Resources:

American Society of Association Executives   www.asaenet.org

American Bus Association- www.aaa.com

Adventure Travel Society- www.adventuretravel.com

Meeting Professionals International www.mpiweb.org

Public Relations society of America (PRSA) www.prsa.org

Travel and Tourism Research Association- www.ttra.com

United States Tour Operators Association www.ustoa.com

Career Opportunities for International Tour Directors

Combine your talents as an International Tour Director with a love of travel and you can travel the world free! As an International Tour Director, you can offer tours anywhere on the globe, and your travel is paid for as part of the tour package. Here are just a few possibilities of tours you can offer groups and individuals:

- Safaris
- Hot Air Ballooning
- Health Spas
- Yoga Retreats
- Honeymoon & Weddings
- Diving
- Casino Tours
- Family Getaways
- Golf Vacations
- Sporting Events
- Cruises
- Special Interest groups
- High Adventure Tours
- Gay & Lesbian Tours & Cruises

Five Key Considerations In Tour Promotion

- Product-Tours: The destination, type of travel
- Customer Target: Niche markets, retirees, adventure groups
- Promotions: Methods in selling your tours and cruises
- Distribution: Selling to groups, associations
- Tour and Cruise Pricing: Where to position the product

Becoming a Dream Merchant!

Tourism has become one of a country's significant industries, providing jobs for thousands of people. Governments and private enterprise support the efforts of International Tour Directors who invest in imaginative and innovative tourist programs. Offering travelers with variety and excitement on their tours is the role of a professional International Tour Director. They sell travelers the dream trip they've always wanted, giving them value for their hard earned money saved toward a trip of a lifetime. International Tour Directors are called upon to design and escort cruises, spa holiday trips, student tours, senior citizen Motor Coach Tours, Incentive programs, conventions – they travel all over the world, whether the event is in London, Paris, New York or Rome.

The International Tour Director with a keen interest in fulfilling the needs of their clients will seek out and find unspoiled and relatively undiscovered corners of the world, where facilities such as superb, uncrowned golf courses, fishing, hiking, splendid scenery, uncluttered roads and hospitable restaurants continue to offer travelers an unforgettable experience. An at the same time they are earning the respect of their associates within the travel industry, they are in earning a comfortable income, enjoy FREE TRAVEL and most of all, Independence!

How to Travel *FREE* As An International Tour Director
By Gerald E. Mitchell

If you're thinking of joining the ranks of professional tour directors, this book is for you! It provides everything you want to know about this career. It will motivate and assist many of you who aspire to travel free while earning a great income! Order it today through Amazon.com or directly from the GEM Group in a handy electronic edition on CD:

Questions and Answers About the Travel-Tourism Industry

Can I work at home full or part-time?

Yes! These days, you have your choice between "Clicks and Bricks" as a workplace – you can work from a home office via the Internet ("Clicks") or in a traditional office setting ("Bricks") -- the choice is yours. Today many tour guide companies and tour operators create an Internet-based business that is operated from home.

I'm very creative and want to promote my interest in being a sole owner. Will I have the opportunity to do so?

Of course. The Travel-Tourism Industry is one of the most dynamic industries anywhere, offering extraordinary opportunities for mobility, creativity, and personal satisfaction.

Can I start out as a Tour Guide and then start my own Destination-Tour Company?

Yes, guiding tours is a good introductory position to the business whether you work for an established tour operator or in other sectors of the travel-tourism industry.

Why is the Travel-Tourism so important to a region or country?

The Travel-Tourism Industry makes commerce, diplomacy, and exchanges of ideas and cultures possible. "The world is becoming a global village," Pope John Paul II told a private audience of travel professional gathered at the Vatican.

In owning a Travel company, what necessary skills are required to be successful?

The list includes all the following:

- Product Development -- Creating exciting and profitable tour programs
- Operations
- Sales and Marketing
- Public Relations
- Administration
- Information technology
- Finance

Where can I acquire additional information on specialized training for the travel-tourism industry?

Many two-year and four-year colleges, universities, and vocational/technical schools have hospitality programs that prepare people to start their own business or move into management positions with in the tour-travel industry.

Chapter 5

Your Road Map to Employment in Travel-Tourism

 Where the Jobs Are

While developing a "blueprint" for a career in the travel-tourism industry, your career plans need to include the following research:

- School Subjects college & universities: what you have studied and will study next
- Working on you personal skills
- Choosing the work environment you desire
- Identifying the minimum educational level for your career choice
- Certification/degrees/certification
- Outlook for the future
- Salaries, perks, benefits, and travel

The great thing about the travel-tourism industry is the flexibility and choices that are offered. The enormous scope of movement between the different sectors of the industry is a vital consideration in view of the uncertainty of today's job market.

Because the travel-tourism industry employs one in ten people worldwide, new employment opportunities for management and supervisors will exceed 45,000 position openings in 2005.

Let's Get Started!

Option #1   You can take the path of least resistance; i.e., perusing the classified ads on Sunday. However, by following the list of guidelines later in this chapter for enhancing your attractiveness and increasing your visibility, you'll begin to tap into that vast majority of jobs that are never advertised -- and you'll be strategically positioned for serious consideration versus having to literally "sell yourself" into a job.

Option #2   To obtain your goal of finding a new job you will have to set yourself daily and weekly goals. Leave home! Conduct field research with your GEM Global career blueprint. Take your notes and go out and conduct site inspections, make appointment and visit members of the travel-tourism industry. Get to know and understand the travel-tourism industry by investigating all the opportunities and career choices available to you.

Option #3 Test the international waters by volunteering in remote corners of the world through volunteer vacation programs.

For High School and College Students ~ A Career Start Challenge

Take Off! Work, study, and volunteer abroad to gain experience and build a "network" of contacts. While seeking short-term work experience, such as teaching English, working is spas, ski, or dive resorts, you'll have the opportunity to focus on learning and establishing mutual understanding between people of many different cultures.

Search the www.goabroad.com website, which is designed for anyone interested in overseas internships, jobs overseas, and free newsletters, and has links to other useful sites such as www.teachabroad.com, www.JobsAbroad.com, and USUniversities.com.

Another useful site that is designed for people wanting to get away www.escapeartist.com, which offers advice and hints for relocating, short-term work, and other channels of information regarding discount airfares and accommodations.

For Adults

Become Involved! Try new career options by volunteering, regardless of the work, which can include teaching practical skills at orphanages, preservation, participating in wild game viewing, and health and environmental education programs for developing countries. Volunteering travel is the fastest growing segment of the global travel industry. "This kind of travel is how you really get to see the world and experience more of the food, the culture, the camaraderie," said a CR-Volunteer Traveler on location in South Africa.

Who to contact:

Turtle Island www.turtlefiji.com

African Conservancy www.aricanconvervancy.org

Micato Safaris www.micato.com

EarthWatch www.earthwatch.org

Habitat for Humanity www.habitat.org

Volunteers for Peace www.vfp.org

Take a Career Step in the Right Direction

Step One: Make a career selection

There are over 400 different career opportunities in the tourism industry, ranging from part-time front-line to executive. You may see a position which offers varied and challenging work. As you learn and gain experience you may be in charge of an entire operation or division and be assigned such tasks as forecasting sales, doing marketing, and conducting training. Gaining this knowledge will offer you the opportunity to own and operate your own travel-tourism business. If you enjoy travel, consider living overseas. The travel-tourism industry is global, and many of the occupations are available around the world.

Step Two: Prepare for Future Training

Research professional trade schools, universities, and community colleges for educational opportunities. Competing for a career in any industry can become fierce, and education and on-the-job training is a MUST. There are many channels you can explore to move your career ahead. Combining both knowledge and practical training can help you to develop a network of contacts and extend the qualifications of your resume. Professional organizations offer workshops, seminars and certification programs.

Step Three: Research Your Career Target

Review and research organizations for training, employment opportunities, and attend career fairs and trade shows.

Step Four: Prepare a Progress Report

List your objectives in a Progress report—a diary of contacts, meetings, events or involvement within the hospitality and tourism industry. Include a note of the number of resumes sent out/follow up dates and with whom.

You will find this resource list invaluable as your career progresses. The contacts you made early when you were just starting out may be the ones who offer you a management position later on.

See the next page for a sample format of a Progress Report.

Step Five: Know Your Product

Conduct site inspections, network and make face-to-face contacts. Interview professionals in the travel-tourism industry to get their perspective on getting started. Who knows? One of them may offer you a job!

Step Six: Attend Travel-Tourism Trade Shows

Attend a trade show, employment mart or other functions sponsored by the travel-tourism industry for networking and employment opportunities. A list of National – International Trade shows is available at in Chapter 7 of this book.

Step Seven: Stick to Your Goals – and Set Goals that Work!

Rather than resolving to learn how to swim, surf or become general manager of a hotel within 30 days, set yourself up to succeed. Ambitious, yet unrealistic, goals leave you frustrated and discouraged. Following 5 simple rules of goal setting to turn good intentions into real life accomplishments. This is the "STICK" method of goal accomplishment.

S *Simple and specific.* Vague and complex goals leave you with a feeling of dread. Keep goals concise and precise.

T *Time-limited.* Have a start and end date. Don't leave it open-ended. To do so is to invite trouble in finishing the goal.

I *Interest.* What you're striving to achieve should interest you, connect with how you live, and your work and your lifestyle. You're most likely to invest in things that truly interest you.

C *Consistent and measurable.* Outline steps and check points. Be able to answer how you're making progress toward your goals by being able to list what you've done to-date.

K *Know-how.* Build on existing strengths and skills to maximize success.

Type of Contact:

❑ Tour Operator/Tour Guide Company/Travel Agent

❑ Cruise Line

❑ Airline/Transport company

❑ Tourism Board

❑ Chamber of Commerce

❑ Local college or university
❑ Technical/Vocational schools

❑ Short-term training opportunities/workshops

❑ Other: _____

Date: _____

Chapter 6

Preparing a Resume That Works!

Your Resume is Your Introduction!

A resume provides the first impression that most employers have of you and your skills. It should be neatly typed on high quality bond (unless, of course, you're sending it electronically via email). At an interview, your portfolio should provide a complete picture of all professional achievements as well as your expertise and an overall personality image. At a minimum, include the following:

Professional Education/Graduate and degree

- Languages: (French, Spanish, other)
- Further Education/Courses/On-the-Job Training
- Employment history
- Facilities, Services, Size of Operation, Level of business

Present & Past Job Responsibilities

- Task Assignments, Scope of Work, and reporting line
- Achievements:
- Improvements, Revenues. Changes, Services implemented
- What you will contribute to the success of the company

Career Accomplishments

- An overview of past job achievements

Professional strengths and special skills

- Identify your field of specialization and expertise
- Future Goals and Career:
- Your plans are as important to you as they are with anyone working with you, directly or indirectly

Other information, Technical and other Skills

- Your additional skills that might be beneficial for upcoming opportunities and could further enhance your profile

Professional membership and affiliations:

- (Refer to the GEM list of organizations and associations, good idea to join a professional group within the travel-tourism industry)
- Special Interests, Hobbies, Activities

References

- List contact or two or more of your past subordinates or staff that worked under your leadership

Compensation Package (expectations)

Other

- Legally permitted to work or having working permit for the following countries (list)
- Relocation and travel preferences
- Choice of contract: open/one year/two years or more

John Doe
132 Main Street
Charleston SC 29418

Email: jdoe@internet.net

Objective: Director of Marketing-North America-Charleston, SC

Professional Experience

Tour Product Manager – 1990-Present
- Negotiated contract rates for major hotel and airlines throughout North America
- Trained sales and marketing staff in 12 major US cities
- Conducted joint sales calls with major hotel and airlines
- Identified and developed revenue-generating year round tour programs for United States and Canada
- Wrote promotional copy that was used in printed-web site and power point presentations
- Establish relationship with national TV and Press Agents
- Conducted national, international FAM tours for Tour Operators and Travel Press

Director of Meeting and Planning Services-1985-1990
- Manage 50 high level conferences and special events
- Travel extensively throughout Europe and Latin American to promote special events and inventive programs for American Express agents.
- Managed accounts with an average budget of 8 million dollars
- Provided $213 million corporate travel-incentive and convention sales

Sample Qualifications
- Computer/Office Skills Word-Power Point, Excel, and Outlook
- Group leadership
- Marketing strategies
- Program management
- Written communications skills
- Sales and Marketing (domestic & International)
- Skilled trainer/presentations/seminars
- Financial leadership

Education
University of New Hampshire (B.A-Hospitality and Tourism)
Additional courses in French, Spanish, and German

Professional affiliations
ASTA
PATA
CLIA

What are your potential employers looking for in a resume?

- ☑ Do you like people?
- ☑ Willing to work week-ends, holidays and into the evening
- ☑ Detailed orientated
- ☑ Good communicator
- ☑ Able to speak a foreign language
- ☑ Be able to think on your feet
- ☑ Prepared to relocate
- ☑ Enrolled at local universities, colleges on distant learning programs

Need help In Making a Career Choice?

Hire a Coach:

Job and Career Transition Coach Service: www.careernetwork.org

Career Counselor

Certified Professional Counselor: www.napsweb.org

Resume Writer

Master Résumé Writer: www.cminstitute.com

Now….Start Marketing Yourself!

Whether you are looking in the future or presently employed but undecided about your career choices, start exploring potential jobs now. After exploring your promotional opportunities you may have realized that you've hit a ceiling with no prospect for new assignments on the horizon. Or maybe you've reviewed the different careers higher education offers and you still haven't found the job that will make your heart sing.

Sell yourself: Regardless of what type of position you're seeking, your job while searching for it is essentially a *sales job*. That is, you are in the business of selling yourself to the marketplace. Of course, depending upon your orientation to the activity of selling things, that could be music to your ears, or it could become a chore.

Despite the obvious logic of all of this, many people are just plain uncomfortable with the idea of having to sell themselves to potential employers. It can feel intimidating, pushy and a bit like swimming upstream to someone who doesn't sell for a living.

However, there are other ways to approach this challenge. Instead of concentrating on traditional means of selling yourself, consider using a two-pronged approach that focuses on enhancing your attractiveness and building visibility in the marketplace.

Enhance your Attraction Level

Developing your sense of self and what your have to offer can help you hone in on a manner of presentation that makes people say, "We can use this person in our company!" The place to begin is learning to enhance your attraction level You can do this effectively by considering what you find attractive in other people.

What positive characteristics, traits and behaviors stand out in others?

A keen level of self-awareness and understanding of their own strengths and weaknesses.

- Knowing what they want and the ability to clearly and concisely articulate what they are seeking.
- They can succinctly describe what they have to offer in terms that minimize jargon.
- Respectful communicators who are interred in others, not just being interested in themselves.
- Optimism and energy.
- Speaking well of former employers.
- Demonstrate imitative and take responsibility for making things happen.
- Take pride in their appearance and display poise and self-confidence.

Now rate yourself. Any gaps you observe represent areas you need to work on. Your goal is to become a magnet that attracts well-connected people and good opportunities in the Travel-Tourism Industry.

Increase your Visibility

Of course, attraction only works if you put yourself in situations where valuable contacts, colleagues and would-be employers are aware that you exist. Step two is to focus on increasing your visibility in the business communities you are interested in infiltrating. Many people encounter difficulties in the job search process not because they are unqualified, but because they are invisible to those who would value their qualifications.

Ideas for increasing your visibility:

- Join clubs, professional associations (travel, hospitality, tourism association listed under "resources :) and civic organizations that are populated by people who are in fields and lines of business your are interested in.

- When you join those groups, take an active role and volunteer for specific assignments. Position yourself for appropriate leadership opportunities.

- Prepare several brief talks that reflect your area of expertise and offer complimentary presentations at breakfast meetings and luncheon groups.

- Volunteer for roles in your church, community and charitable organizations that offer exposure. You'll benefit from doing well.

- Write articles for newsletters, bulletins and professional publications related to your field.

Great Websites to Post Your Resume!

Over 25,000 employment positions are posted weekly "worldwide." The following websites are excellent places to post your resume.

www.jobshadow.org

www.resortjobs.com

www.hcareers.com

www.hospitalitycareers.com

www.hospitalitycentures.com

www.travelmanagement.com

www.tourismcareers.com

Totaljobs.com/travel-job.htmlwwwtypefocus.com

www.toutismhrc.com

www.atto.org

www.careerage.com

www.careerfitter.com

www.otto.igs/net

www.hoteljobresource.com

www.foodservice.com

www.benchmarkhospitality.com

www.hoteljobresource.com

Chapter 7

Resources Within the Tourism Industry

Launching Your Career

Travel-Tourism training is essential in today's job market. Competition can be tough, and having a degree or additional training in your field is key to a successful career. Public and private universities, tech schools and colleges offer a wide variety of programs. Also available are distance-learning educational programs offered by top universities around the world. On-The Job Training in any industry is an asset. You will be required to have on-the-job experience within the travel-tourism industry. Benefits of such training will help you gain a better understanding of the business and decide which direction you want to take.

Using the Internet, you can find sources for:

- Scholarships
- Internship
- In-house training program
- Apprenticeship
- Technical Colleges
- Universities/Colleges
- Training programs and seminars-
- Trade Shows-Career Fairs

Each website offers a wealth of sources to start your on your tourism career. It is important to select an official accredited course.

Columbia Southern University

Hospitality and Tourism BS degree program

Columbia Southern University has developed a Distance Learning University. CSU is an accredited member of DETC, the Accrediting Commission of the Distance Education and Training Council (www.detc.org) and is a recognized member of the Council for Higher Education Accreditation. CSU is an accredited, degree-granting member of the DETC and licensed by the Department of Education, State of Alabama. You will find that CSU's courses and project assignments are designed to allow you to incorporate work-related issues, so that your learning will have an immediate impact on your career.

www.columbiasouthern.edu

1-800-977-8449 or 251-981-3771

Recommended Industry Resources- Hotel-Hospitality Industry

American Hospitality Academy (AHA)

www.americanhospitalityacademy.com

The American Hospitality Academy (AHA) develops future hospitality leaders while fostering international understanding among trainees and the American public. The American Hospitality Academy is proud to have championed a practical training and internship program that teaches both cultural awareness and leadership skills that are necessary to be successful in a global service economy. The American Hospitality Academy began providing structured training opportunities for students in 1986 and maintains and established international cultural exchange program. AHA is designated by the Department of State as a sponsor of an Exchange Visitor Program in accordance with the administrative regulations issued under the Mutual Education and Cultural Exchange Act of 1961.

Through AHA's structured programs, trainees (Cultural Ambassadors) share their culture through practical training, learn ethics and work values while developing leadership skills. AHA encourages everyone to learn and embrace different ways of life as our global existence depends on learning to live harmoniously together without the threat of violence and conflict.

American Hotel & Lodging Education Foundation

www.ahlf.org

The scholarship program supports the educational development of students pursing hospitality-related undergraduate degrees in U.S. colleges and universities. AH&LEF has disbursed more than $3.5 million dollars since its inception. Last year, the Foundation distributed $476,000 to 330 students and hospitality professionals.

American Society of Travel Agents (ASTA)-www.astanet.com

An excellent source for those considering opening their own business

Mature Adult Travel Specialist Course

By Talula Guntner, CTC, MCC

Every eight seconds someone in the United States turns 50. Mature adults (50+ years old) control 50% of discretionary spending. That's what makes this such a lucrative, growing niche. Course topics include:

- **Expectations, demands and travel trends of mature adults**
- Travel patterns and expenditures
- The different buying patterns of the senior citizen (65+) and baby boomer (50-64) markets
- "Hot Buttons" for upscale mature adults

- Unique marketing and sales strategies
- Companies sensitive to mature adult needs
- Health and the mature traveler

USA Travel Expert Program

By Sue Wilder, CTC

Designed for international travel professionals to develop an expertise about the United States of America (USA) as a tourist destination and enhance their service for inbound travel for clients living outside of the United States (US). This is great opportunity for travel professionals in the international arena to become "experts" on selling the USA.

While there is no substitute for personally experiencing all that the United States has to offer, this program will lay a foundation of essential knowledge upon which to develop a comprehensive specialty in travel to the United States. Topics include:

- Identification of trends and characteristics of the United States inbound travel industry.
- Essential information about regulatory and other practical issues regarding travel to the United States Discuss relevant aspects of the country's transportation, accommodations, dining and culture. Identify basic geographical characteristics of the United States.
- Highlights of key features of destinations in nine major touring regions of the United States: Northeast, Mid-Atlantic, South, Great Lakes, Great Plains, West, Northwest, Hawaii and Alaska.
- Tips for visiting popular destinations throughout the United States.
- Earn a certificate designating you as an ASTA USA Travel Expert.

Family Travel Specialist Course

by Sue Wilder, CTC

The family travel market is growing and diversifying. This course takes a focused look at the different types of families, their buying patterns and how their needs evolve as they progress through the family life cycle. Topics include:

- Defining the family travel marketplace

- Addressing the unique needs of various types of families
- Planning the family vacation: do's & don'ts
- Identifying family-oriented operators and destinations

Niche Travel Specialist Course

by Robin Fetsch, CTC

This course examines a wide diversity of special interest groups. Topics include how to conduct local research and positioning, as well as promoting and selling special interest travel. More than 100 areas of specialization are discussed including:

- Eco-tourism
- Wine/Gourmet
- Historical/Cultural
- Disabled
- Scuba Diving
- Spa/Fitness
- Dude Ranch
- Spiritual/Religious
- Sports
- Gay & Lesbian

Chapter 8

Travel-Tourism Career Resource Guide

An Alphabetical Guide to Career Resources

A

Adventure Recreation

http://www. National OutdoorLeaderSchool.com and

http://www.Outwardbound

The Wilderness Association

Rte. #1, Box 3400, Driggs, Idaho 83422

Adventure and Outdoor Travel

www.gorp.com

www.iexplore.com

www.away.com

Airline pilot

Contact the following organizations for information on becoming an airline pilot:

Airline Pilots Association, International

Web: http://www.alpa.org

Airlines/Airport Management: American Association of Airport Executives

Http://www.airport net.org

American Society of Association Executives

http://www.asaenet.org

American Hospitality Academy

www.americanhospitalityacademy.com

American Hotel & Lodging Educational Foundation

www.ahlf.org

Aviation Careers

www.aviationcareer.net

B

Bartender

http://www.americanbartender.org

Beverage service (alcohol) training programs

http://www.nraef.org

Bed & Breakfast

Innkeeper employment and ownership

http://www.paii.org

http://www.newenglandinns.com

C

College of Aeronautics, La Guardia Airport

http://www.aero.edu

Career books -- information about high schools students membership, national forums, job fairs, contacts

http://www.jet-jobs.com

Concierge Career

Les Clefs d'Or USA

http://www.lesclefsdorusa.com

International Concierge Institute (ICI)

http://www.concierge-institute.com

Chefs & Cooks

American Culinary Federation   http://www.acfchefs.org

American Institute of Baking   http://www.aibonline.org

Culinary Institute of America   http://www.ciachef.edu

Canadian Federation of Chefs and Cooks   http://www.cfcc.ca

Cruise Ships employment

Official Trade Organization: Cruise Line International Association

http://www.cruising.org

Cruise Services International Employment opportunities

Web: http://www.cruisedreamjob.com

Cruise ships list

http://www.cruiselinejobs.com

E

Educational Institute of American Hotel and Lodging Association

For internships, scholarships, or certification   http://www.ei-ahla.org

Education Systems/The Center for Travel Education

www.icta.com

Other Education

Travel Agency Training   www.boydschool.com

Hospitality-Hotels Training   www.ei-ahma.org

Housekeeper Programs Training

International Executive Housekeepers Association

http://www.ieha.org

Employment

http://www.hcareers.com offers over 56,000 jobs world-wide.

On this site you can seek out job opportunities in restaurants, catering, casinos, travel, resorts, chef, spa and all food service jobs -- for all hotel, restaurant, retail and hospitality industry professionals seeking a career as a hotel manager, restaurant manager, retail manager, chef, culinary specialist, or travel agent with careers from entry-level to senior management world-wide.

E-Commerce Employment Opportunities Resources

1Travel.com   http://www.1Travel.com

Interactive Travel Services Association   http://www.interactive travel.org

WebTravel News   http://www.webtravelnews.com

Amadeus   http://www.Amadeus.net

Employment-Hospitality Industry

Hcareers.com

www.hcareers.com

www.hotelrecruiters.com

www.hospitalityrecruiters.com

http://careers.marriott.com//

http://jobsearch.marriott.newjobs.com

www.coolworks.com

www.aeps.com (Aviation employment)

www.cruising.org (Cruise Line employment)

www.hsmai.org (Sales & Marketing/Hospitality)

www.prsa.org (Public Relations)

www.hospitalitylink.com

www.hospitalityonline.com

www.americanhospitalityacademy.com/homepage.html

www.acinet.org (international and national employment opportunities –excellent site!

F

Federal Aviation Administration (FAA)

http://www.faa.gov

Flight attendants

Site for jobs, and other aviation-related sites Web: http://www.flightattendants.org

H

Higher Education-Employment Travel-Hospitality-Tourism Industry

Food service industry

For jobs, accredited education programs

International Council on Hotel, Restaurant, and Institutional Education

http://www.chrie.org

Hospitality/Hotel School Programs

Web: http://www.chrie.org

I

International Newspapers:

www.ecola.com

www.naa.or/hotlink/index.asp

www.mediainfo.com/emedia

M

Meeting & Planners: Society of Incentive & Travel Executives   www.site-intly.org

International Festivals &Events Association

Maps:

www.mapquest.com

www.indo.com/distance

Country Information maps:

www.odci.gov/cia

N

National Restaurant Association Educational Foundation   Scholarships, and careers

http://www.nraef.org

Canadian Society of Nutrition Management

http://www.csnm.org

National Academy Foundation

www.naf-education.org

P

Public Relations Society of America (PRSA)   www.prsa.org

R

Research-Resources Travel-Tourism Industry

     Data collection: World Tourism Organization

     Capitan Haya 42

     28020 Madrid Spain

     http://www.world-tourism.org

Resort Work

     The Aspen Skiing Company

     www.aspensnowmass.com

Club Med

     http://clubmed.cpm

Resort Jobs

     http://www.resortjobs.com

Resorts:/Campgrounds: American Resort Development Association   www.arda.org

National Association of RV Parks & Campgrounds

Professional Association of Innkeepers International   www.paii.org/index.html

S_____

Spas

www.spafinder.com

www.spa.com

Student opportunities-Ski Employment opportunities

The Student & Youth Travel association of North America   www.syta.com

Sales and Marketing - Hospitality-Tourism

For sales and marketing career in the hospitality industry contact;

http://www.hsmai.org

Seasonal jobs: Cool Works   http://www.coolworks.com

Ski Resort Employment opportunities:

National Ski Area Association: http://www.nsaa.org

 Professional Ski Instructors of America   http://www.psia.org

Certification for the ski industry: University of Maine   http://www.umf.maine.edu/-ski

Ski Instructor and other employment opportunities:

Aspen Skiing Company: www.aspensnowmass.com

Study Abroad:

www.Transitionsabroad.com

www.goabroad.com

www.globalexchange.org

www.globalvolunteers.org

www.ciee.org

www.escapeartist.com

www.travelearn.com

www.learn.unh.edu

www.iagora.com

T

Theme Parks

www.disney.go.com

Travel Warnings:

http://www.travel.state.gov

www.airsecurity.com/hotspotsHOTSPOTS.asp

Tour Operators-Adventure

www.gordonguide.com

www.travelon.com

www.greentravel.com

Tour Operators: Spa, Diving, Surfing

www.islands.com

www.surfline.com

www.diverplanet.com

Tour Operators-Golf

www.golfonline.com/travel

www.golf-travel.com

Tour Operators-Cycling

www.sycling.org/

Tour Operators-Mountaineering

www.mountainzone.com

Tour Operators-Skiing

www.goski.com

www.skinet.com

Tour Operators-Honeymooning

www.honeymoon.com

www.honeymoontravel-htr.com

Tour Operators-Luxury Travel

www.luxurytravel.com

www.luxury4less.com

www.luxelife.com

www.harperassociates.com

www.luxurylink.com

Tour Operator-Specialty Travel

www.specialtytravel.com

www.infohub.com

www.shawguides.com

www.specialtyworldtravel.com

Tour Guide

United States Tour Operators Association

Web: http://www.ustoa.com

The GEM Group

Web: http://www.thegemgroup.org

Travel Writers

www.travelwriters.com

Inkspot

www.inkspot.com/genres/travel/market.html

Travel Agent

Employment in the Travel Industry

American Society of Travel Agents

Web: http://www.astanet.com

Institute of Certified Travel Agents

Web: http//www.icta.com

Tour Guides

Interpretive, Eco-Heritage-Heritage-Cultural Tour Guide

Nature and Eco-Travel and resources

International eco-tourism Society

Web: http://www.ecotourism.org

Tour Guide Outdoor activities (Adventure Guiding etc.)

Outdoor Industry Association

3775 Iris Avenue, Suite 5

Boulder, CO 80301

http://www.outdoorindustry.org

Outward Bound-USA

http://www.outwordbound.org

How to be a Tour Guide

The GEM Group: www.thegemgroup.org

Travel Books

www.hotwired.com/rough

www.frommers.com

www.fodors.com

www.lonelyplanet.com

International Trade Administration Office of Travel & Tourism Industries

www.tinet.ita.doc.gov

International Council on Hotel, Restaurant and Institutional Education

www.chrie.org

International Association of Scientific Experts in Tourism

www.aiest.org

International Association of Convention & Visitor Bureaus

www.iacvb.org

The National Society of Minorities in Hospitality

www.msmh.org

The Society for Accessible Travel and Hospitality

www.sath.org

Publishers-Consultants-Travel-Tourism Industry

www.thegemgroup.org

United States Tour Operators Association

www.ustoa.com

National Tour Association

www.ntaonline.com

Multicultural Food Service & Hospitality Alliance

www.mfha.net

The Travel Institute

www.thetravelinstitute.com

Travel and Tourism Research Association

www.ttra.com

U.S. Department of State

www.state.gov/travel

American Society of Travel Agents

www.astanet.com

Tourism Offices Worldwide

www.towd.com

Organizers of Group Tours Trade Shows and Conferences

Local Chamber of Commerce: Join your local chamber of commerce for a list of contacts and marketing opportunities for your tours and services.

US Chamber of Commerce: Worldchamberdirectory@compurserve.com: Will promote your services abroad.

United State Travel Council: Contact U.S. Department of Commerce, International Trade Administration, Trade Development, Tourism Industries, Washington, D.C. 20230; Phone; (202) 482-4029 for information on all of the information available from Tourism Industries, visit the web site at http://tinet.ita.doc.gov.

Greyline Sightseeing Tours: www.greylinetours.com: List rates and services for tours within the United States and around the world. Excellent source of tours and prices.

Leisure Group Travel: www.leisuregrouptravel.com excellent resource and opportunity to promote your tours and services.

International Association of Convention & Visitors Bureaus-IACVB

2000 L St., NW

Suite 702

Washington, DC 20036-4990

United Bus Owners of America:

1300 L Ave. NW

Suite 1050

Washington, DC 2000 4107

1-800-424-8262

Government and State Tourism Offices

The importance of working with government and state tourist offices is being able to acquire additional information on a destination. Aside from the general information that is readily available, certain department heads will offer advice on planning tour itineraries and recommend qualified land operator/step-on guide services, hotels and transportation companies. For planning a group function, the government or state tourist office will make available films and slides subject to their budget and the nature of the group function, and will sometimes offer a guest speaker knowledgeable on the destination being promoted.

Alaska

Alaska Travel Industry Association

2600 Cordova Street, Ste. 201

Anchorage, AK 99503

E-mail: info@alaskatia.org

Web site: http://www.travelalaska.com/

Arizona

1110 West Washington, Suite 155

Phoenix, AZ 85007

(602) 364-3700 or (866) 275-5816

Web site: http://www.arizonaguide.com

Arkansas

Arkansas Department of Parks & Tourism Office

1 Capitol Mall

Little Rock, AR 72201

(800) 628-8725 or (501) 682-7777

Web site: http://www.arkansas.com

California

California Office of Tourism

(800) 462-2543 or (800)TO-CALIFORNIA

Email: caltour@commerce.ca.gov

Web site: http://www.gocalif.ca.gov

Colorado

Colorado Tourism Office

1625 Broadway, Ste. 1700

Denver, CO 80202

(800) 265-6726

Web site: http://www.colorado.com

Connecticut

Connecticut Tourism

(800) 282-6863

Email: German.Rivera@po.state.ct.us

Web site: http://www.tourism.state.ct.us/

District of Columbia

Washington Convention and Visitors Association

901 7th Street NW, 4th Floor

Washington, DC 20001-3719

(202) 789-7000

Fax: (202) 789-7037

Web site: http://www.washington.org

Delaware

Delaware Tourism Office

99 Kings Highway, Box 1401

Dover, DE 19903

(866) 284-7483 or (302) 739-4271

Fax: (302) 739-5749

Web site: http://www.visitdelaware.com

Florida

Florida Division of Tourism

661 East Jefferson Street, Suite 300

Tallahassee, Florida 32301

(888) 735-2872

Web site: http://www.flausa.com/

Georgia

Georgia Department of Industry, Trade & Tourism

Tel: (800) 847-4842

Web site: http://www.georgia.org

Hawaii

Hawaii Visitors Bureau

Waikiki Business Plaza

2270 Kalakaua Ave #801

Honolulu, HI 96815

(800) 464-2924 or (808) 923-1811

Fax: (808) 922-8991

Email: info@hvcb.org

Web site: http://www.gohawaii.com

Idaho

Idaho Department of Commerce

Division of Tourism Development

700 West State Street

P.O. Box 83720

Boise, ID 83720-0093

(208) 334-2470

Fax: (208) 334-2631

Web site: http://www.visitid.org/

Illinois

Illinois Bureau of Tourism

100 West Randolph #3-400

Chicago, IL 60601

1-800-2CONNECT

Email: Tourism@illinoisbiz.biz

Web site: http://www.enjoyillinois.com

Indiana

Indiana Tourism Division

1 North Capitol Ave #700

Indianapolis, IN 46204

1-800-ENJOY-IN

Fax:317-233-6887

Email: webmaster@enjoyindiana.com

Web site: http://www.in.gov/enjoyindiana/

Iowa

Iowa Department of Tourism

200 East Grand Ave.

Des Moines, IA 50309

888-472-6035

Fax: 515-242-4718

Email: tourism@ided.state.ia.us.

Web site: httphttp://www.traveliowa.com/

Kansas

Kansas Travel and Tourism Division

1000 S.W. Jackson Street, Suite 100

Topeka, Kansas 66612-1354

1-800-2KANSAS

Fax: (913) 296-5055

Email: travtour@kansascommerce.com

Web site: http://www.travelks.com

Kentucky

Kentucky Department of Travel Development Visitors Information Service

500 Mero St

Frankfort, KY 40601

(800) 225-8747 or (502) 564-4930

Fax: (502) 564-5695

Web site: http://www.kytourism.com

Louisiana

Louisiana Office of Tourism

(800) 33-GUMBO or (225) 342-8100

Fax: (225) 342-8390

Email: free.info@crt.state.la.us

Web site: http://www.louisianatravel.com

Maine

Maine Office of Tourism

#59 State House Station

Augusta, ME 04333-0059

1-888-624-6345

Web site: http://www.visitmaine.com/

Maryland

Maryland Office of Tourism Development

217 East Redwood St, 9th Floor

Baltimore, MD 21202

(800) 634-7386

Web site: http://www.mdisfun.org

Massachusetts

Massachusetts Office of Travel and Tourism

10 Park Plaza, Suite 4510

Boston, MA 02116

(800) 227-MASS or (617) 973-8500

Email: VacationInfo@state.ma.us

Web site: http://www.mass-vacation.com/

Michigan

Michigan Travel Bureau

300 N. Washington Square, 2nd Floor

Lansing, Michigan 48913

(888) 78-GREAT or (517) 373-0670

Fax: (517) 373-0059

Web site: http://travel.michigan.org

Minnesota
Minnesota Office of Tourism
100 Metro Square, 121 7th Place E.
St. Paul, MN 55101
(800) 657-3700 or (612) 296-5029
Email: explore@state.mn.us
Web site: http://www.exploreminnesota.com

Mississippi
Mississippi Division of Tourism Development
Post Office Box 849
Jackson, MS 39205
(866) 733-6477 or (601) 359.3297
Fax: (601) 359-5757
Email: lturnage@mississippi.org
Web site: http://www.visitmississippi.net

Missouri
Missouri Division of Tourism
Post Office Box 1055
Jefferson City, MO 65102
(800) 810-5500 or (573) 751-4133
Fax: (573) 751-5160
Web site: http://www.missouritourism.org

Montana
Travel Montana
Post Office Box 200533
Helena, MT 59620
(800) 847-4868 or (406) 841-2870
Fax: (406) 841-2871
Web site: http://www.visitmt.com

Nebraska
Nebraska Division of Travel & Tourism
Post Office Box 98907
Lincoln, NE 68509
1-877-NEBRASKA
Email: tourism@visitnebraska.org
Web site: http://www.visitnebraska.org/

Nevada
Nevada Commission on Tourism
401 North Carson Street
Carson City, NV 89701
(800) 638-2328 or (775) 687-4322
Fax: (775) 687-6779
Email: ncot@travelnevada.com
Web site: http://www.travelnevada.com

New Hampshire
New Hampshire Office of Travel and Tourism
PO Box 1856
Concord NH 03302-1856
1-800-FUN-IN-NH or (603) 271-2665
Fax: (603) 271-6870
Email: travel@dred.st.nh.us
Web site: http://www.visitnh.gov/

New Jersey
New Jersey Commerce & Economic Growth Commission P.O. Box 820
Trenton, NJ 08625-0820
1-800-VISIT-NJ or (609) 777- 0885
Web site: http://www.state.nj.us/travel

New Mexico
New Mexico Department of Tourism
491 Old Santa Fe Trail
Santa Fe, NM 87503
(800) 733-6396 ext 0643
Fax: (505) 827-7402
Web site: http://www.newmexico.org/

New York
New York State Travel Info Center
1 Commerce Plaza
Albany, NY 12245
(800) 225-5697
Web site: http://www.iloveny.state.ny.us

North Carolina
North Carolina State Board of Tourism
301 North Wilmington St.
Raleigh, NC 27601
(800) VISIT NC or (919) 733-8372
Fax: (919) 715-3097
Web site: http://www.visitnc.com

North Dakota
North Dakota Tourism Division
Century Center
1600 E. Century Ave. Suite 2
PO Box 2057
Bismarck, N.D. 58503
(800) 435-5663 or (701) 328-2525
Fax: (701) 328-4878
Email: tourism@state.nd.us
Web site: http://www.ndtourism.com

Ohio

Ohio Division of Travel and Tourism

77 S. High St., 29th Floor

Columbus, OH 43215

(800) 282-5393

Web site: http://www.ohiotourism.com

Oklahoma

Oklahoma Tourism And Recreation Department

Travel & Tourism Division

15 N. Robinson, Suite 801

PO Box 52002

Oklahoma City, OK 73152-2002

(800) 652-6552 or (405)521-2406

Fax: (405)521-3992

Email: information@TravelOK.com

Web site: http://www.travelok.com

Oregon

Oregon Tourism Commission

775 Summer St NE

Salem, OR 97310

(800) 547-7842 or (503) 986-0000

Fax: (503) 986-0001

Email: info@traveloregon.com

Web site: http://www.traveloregon.com

Pennsylvania

Pennsylvania Department of Community and Economic Development

Office of Tourism, Film and Economic Development Marketing

4th Floor, Commonwealth Keystone Building

400 North Street

Harrisburg, PA 17120-0225 USA

(800) 237-4363 or (717) 787-5453

Fax: (717) 787-0687

Web site: http://www.experiencepa.com

Rhode Island

Rhode Island Tourism Division

1 West Exchange Street

Providence, RI 02903

800-556-2484

(401) 222-2601

Fax: (401) 273-8720

Email: visitrhodeisland@riedc.com

Web site: http://www.visitrhodeisland.com/

South Carolina

South Carolina Department of Parks, Recreation and Tourism

1205 Pendleton Street

Columbia, South Carolina 29201

(803) 734-1700

Fax: (803) 273-8270

Web site: http://www.discoversouthcarolina.com

South Dakota

South Dakota Department of Tourism

711 East Wells Ave

Pierre, SD 57501

(800) 732-5682 or (605) 773-3301

Fax: (605) 773-3256

E-mail: sdinfo@state.sd.us

Web site: http://www.travelsd.com

Tennessee

Tennessee Tourism Division

Wm. Snodgrass/Tennessee Tower

312 8th Avenue North, 25th Floor

Nashville, TN 37243

(800) 836-6200 or (615) 741-2159

Web site: http://www.tnvacation.com/

Texas

Texas Department of Tourism

Post Office Box 12728

Austin, TX 78711

(800) 888-8839 or (512) 462-9191

Web site: http://www.traveltex.com

Utah

Utah Travel Council

Council Hall

300 North State

Salt Lake City, UT 84114

1-800 UTAH-FUN, (800) 200-1160 or (801) 538-1030

Web site: http://www.utah.com

Vermont

Vermont Dept. of Tourism and Marketing

6 Baldwin St., Drawer 33

Montpelier, VT 05633-1301

(800) 837-6668 or (802) 828-3676

E-mail: info@VermontVacation.com

Web site: http://www.travel-vermont.com

Virginia

Virginia Tourism Corporation

901 E. Byrd Street

Richmond, VA 23219

(800) VISIT VA

Email:VAinfo@helloinc.com

Web site: http://www.virginia.org

Washington

Washington State Tourism (800) 544-1800

Web site: http://www.tourism.wa.gov

West Virginia

West Virginia Division of Tourism

90 MacCorkle Ave. SW

South Charleston WV 25303

(800) 225-5982 or (304) 558-2200

Web site: http://www.wva.state.wv.us/callwva/

Wisconsin

Wisconsin Department of Tourism

201 West Washington Avenue

PO Box 8690

Madison WI 53708-8690

(800) 432-8747 or (608) 266-2161

Email: tourinfo@travelwisconsin.com

Web site: http://www.travelwisconsin.com

Wyoming

Wyoming Division of Tourism

I-25 at College Dr

Cheyenne, WY 82002

(800) 225-5996 or (307) 777-7777

Fax: (307) 777-2877

International Tourism Offices

Web site: http://www.wyomingtourism.org

Anguilla

Anguilla Tourist Information

c/o Medhurst & Associates, Inc.

271 Main Street

Northport, NY 11768

(800) 553-4939

Web Site: http://net.ai/

Antigua

Antigua & Barbuda Department of Tourism & Trade

610 Fifth Avenue #311

New York, NY 10020

1-888-268-4227

FAX: (212) 757-1607

E-MAIL: info@antigua-barbuda.org

Web Site: http://www.antigua-barbuda.org/

Argentina

National Tourist Council

12 West 56th Street

New York, NY 10019

(212) 603-0443

FAX: (212) 315-5545

Web site: http://www.sectur.gov.ar

Aruba

Aruba Tourism Authority

1000 Harbor Blvd.

Weehawken, NJ 07087

(800) TO-ARUBA

(201) 330-0800, (212) 246-3030

FAX: (201) 330-8757

E-MAIL: atanjix@aruba.com

Web Site: http://www.olmco.com/aruba/

Australia

Australian Tourist Commission

1601 Massachusetts Ave NW

Washington, DC 20036

(202) 797-3000

FAX: (202) 797-3100

Web Site: www.australia.com

Australian Tourist Commission

Century Plaza Towers

2049 Century Plaza East

Los Angeles, CA 90067

(310) 229-4870

Web Site: www.australia.com

Austria

Austrian National Tourist Office

P.O. Box 1142- Times Square

New York, NY 10108-1142

(212) 944-6880

Web Site (North America): http://www.anto.com/

Web Site (International): http://austria-info.at/content.html

Bahamas

Bahamas Tourist Office

150 East 52nd Street

New York, NY 10022

(800) 422-4262

(212) 758-2777

FAX: (212) 753-6531

Bahamas Tourist Office

3450 Wilshire Blvd. #208

Los Angeles, CA 90010

(800) 439-6993

Web Site: http://www.interknowledge.com/bahamas/main.html

Barbados

Barbados Tourism Authority

800 Second Avenue

New York, NY 10017

(800) 221-9831, (212) 986-6516

FAX: (212) 573-9850

Web Site: http://www.barbados.org/

Belgium

Belgian Tourist Office

780 Third Avenue

New York, NY 10017

(212) 758-8130

FAX: (212) 355-7675

Email: info@visitbelgium.com

Website: edhttp://www.visitbelgium.com

Belize

Belize Tourism Board

New Central Bank Building, Level 2

Gabourel Lane

P.O. Box 325

Belize City, Belize

Tel: 011-501-2-31913 or

1-800-624-0686

Fax: 011-501-2-31943

Email: info@travelbelize.org

Websites: http://www.travelbelize.org and http://www.belizetourism.org

Bermuda

Bermuda Department of Tourism

310 Madison Avenue

New York, NY 10017

(800) 223-6106, (212) 818-9800

Web Site: http://www.bermudatourism.com/

Bonaire

Bonaire Tourist Board

10 Rockefeller Plaza

New York, NY 10020

(212) 956-5911

Web Site: http://www.infobonaire.com

British Virgin Islands

British Virgin Islands Tourist Board

370 Lexington Avenue

New York, NY 10017

(800) 835-8530, (212) 696-0400

FAX: (212) 949-8254

British Virgin Islands Tourist Board

1804 Union Street

San Francisco, CA 94123

(415) 775-0344

FAX: (415) 775-2554

Web Site: http://bviwelcome.com

Bulgaria

Bulgarian Tourist Information Center

1170 Broadway Room 611

New York, NY 10017

(212) 252-9277

e-mail: btc2000@earthlink.net

Web site info: www.btc2000.com

Caribbean

Caribbean Tourism Organization

80 Broad St. 32nd Floor

New York, NY 10017

(212) 635-9530

FAX: (212) 635-9511

Web Site: http://www.doitcaribbean.com

Cayman Islands

Cayman Islands Tourist Office

6100 Blue Lagoon

Miami, FL 33126

(800) 327-8777

FAX: (305) 267-2931

Web Site: http://www.caymans.com

Cayman Islands Tourist Office

3440 Wilshire Blvd. Ste. 1202

Los Angeles, CA 90010

(213) 738-1968

FAX: (213) 738-1829

Web Site: http://www.caymans.com

Chile

Chilean National Tourist Board

Sernatur

Avenue Providencia 1550

Santiago, Chile

(800) CHILE 66 (Automated)

Fax: 001-562-251-8469

Web Site: http://www.segegob.cl/sernatur/inicio.html

China

China National Tourist Office

350 Fifth Avenue Rm #6413

New York, NY 10018

(212) 760-1710 (Automated), 212-760-8218

FAX: 212-760 8809

www.cnta.com

China National Tourist Office

333 West Broadway #3201

Glendale, CA 91204

(818) 545-7505 (Automated), 818-545-7507

FAX: 818 -545 7506

www.cnta.com

Cook Islands

Cook Islands Tourist Authority

5757 Century Blvd. Suite #660

Los Angeles, CA 90045

(310)641-5621

Costa Rica

Costa Rica National Tourist Board

P. O. Box 12766-1000

San Jose, Costa Rica

(800) 343-6332, (506) 222-1090 or 223-1733, ext. 277

Fax: (506)257-6325-5452

Web Site: http://www.tourism-costarica.com

Cuba

Cubatur

Calle 23 #156

Vedado, Habana

Cuba

Curacao

Curacao Tourist Board

7951 SW 6th St., Ste. 216

Plantation, FL 33324

Toll Free: (800) 328-7222

Web Site: http://www.curacao-tourism.com

Cyprus

Cyprus Tourism

13 East 40th Street

New York, NY 10016

Tel: (212) 683-5280

Fax: (212) 683-5282

Email: gocyprus@aol.com

Web Site: http://www.cyprustourism.org

Czech & Slovak Republics
Czech & Slovak Service Center
1511 K Street NW, Suite 1030
Washington, DC 20005
(202) 638-5505
FAX: (202) 638-5308
Email: cztc@cztc.demon.co.uk
Web Site: http://www.czech-slovak-tourist.co.uk/index.html

Denmark
Scandinavian National Tourist Offices
655 Third Avenue
New York, NY 10017
(212) 885-9700
Web Site: http://www.goscandinavia.com

Dominica
Dominica Tourist Office
800 Second Ave
New York, New York 10017
(212) 599-8478
FAX (212) 808-4975
Email: dmaun@undp.org

Dominican Republic
Dominican Republic Tourist Office
2355 Falzedo St. Suite 307
Coral Gables, FLA
(888) 358-9594; (305) 444-4592
FAX: (305) 444-4845

Egypt

Egyptian Tourist Authority

630 Fifth Ave #1706

New York, NY 10111

(212) 332-2570

FAX: (212) 956-6439

Web Site: http://touregypt.net

Egyptian Tourist Authority

8383 Wilshire Blvd #215

Beverly Hills, CA 90211

(213) 653-8815

FAX: (213) 653-8961

Web Site: http://touregypt.net

England

(See Great Britain Tourist Authority)

Europe

European Travel Commission

1 Rockefeller Plaza, Room 214

New York, NY 10020

(212) 218-1200

FAX: (212) 218-1205

E-MAIL: DNMCO@aol.com

Web Site: http://www.visiteurope.com

Fiji

Fiji Visitors Bureau

5777 Century Blvd #220

Los Angeles, CA 90045

(800) 932-3454, (310) 568-1616

FAX: (310) 670-2318

E-MAIL: infodesk@bulafiji-americas.com

Web Site: http://www.fijifvb.gov.fj

Finland

Finnish Tourist Board

655 Third Avenue

New York, NY 10017

(800) 346-4636

(212) 949-2333

FAX: (212) 983-5260

Web Site: http://www.mek.fi/

France

French Government Tourist Office

444 Madison Ave

New York, NY 10022

212-838-7800

Email:info@frenchtourism.com

French Government Tourist Information Line

(900) 990-0040 ($.95/minute)

Web Site: http://www.francetourism.com/

French Government Tourist Office

9454 Wilshire Blvd. #715

Los Angeles, CA 90212

(310) 271-2358

Web Site: http://www.francetourism.com/

French Government Tourist Office

676 North Michigan Ave. Ste 3360

Chicago, IL 60611-2819

(312) 751-7800

FAX: (312) 337-6339

Web Site: http://www.francetourism.com/

French West Indies

(Guadeloupe, St. Barts, St. Martin)

(See French Government Tourist Office)

Germany

German National Tourist Office

122 E 42nd St. 52nd Floor

New York, NY 10168

(212) 661-7200

FAX: (212) 661-7174

E-MAIL: gntony@aol.com

Web site: http://www.germany-tourism.de/

Great Britain

(England, Scotland, Wales, Northern Ireland)

British Tourist Authority 551 5th Ave #701

New York, NY 10176

(800) 462-2748, (212) 986-2200

FAX: (212) 986-1188

Email: travelinfo@bta.org.uk

Web Site: http://www.visitbritain.com/

Greek National Tourist Office

645 Fifth Ave

New York, NY 10022

(212) 421-5777

FAX: (212) 826-6940

Grenada

Grenada Board of Tourism

800 Second Ave, Suite 400K

New York, NY 10017

(800) 927-9554, (212) 687-9554

FAX: (212) 573-9731

Web Site: http://www.grenada.org

Guam

Guam Visitors Bureau - North America

1336-C Park Street

Alameda, CA 94501

phone: 510.865.0366

toll free 1.800.873.4826

fax: 510.865.5165

e-mail: guam@avisoinc.com

Web Site: www.visitguam.org

Guatemala

Guatemalan Tourist Commission

299 Alhambra Circle #510

Miami, FL 33134

(305) 442-0651

Honduras

Honduras Tourist Office

P.O. Box 140458

Coral Gables, FL 33114

(800) 410-9608

FAX: (305)461-0602

E-MAIL: 104202.3433@compuserve.com

Web Site: http://www.hondurasinfo.hn

Hong Kong

Hong Kong Tourist Association

590 Fifth Ave

New York, NY 10036

(212) 869-5008

FAX: (212) 730-2605

E-MAIL: hktanyc@aol.com

Web Site: http://www.hkta.org

Hong Kong Tourist Association

10940 Wilshire Blvd #1220

Los Angeles, CA 90024

(310) 208-4582

FAX: (310) 208-1869

E-MAIL: hktalax@aol.com

Web Site: http://www.hkta.org

Hungary

Hungarian Tourist Board

150 East 58th Street

New York, NY 10510-0001

(212) 355-0240

Email: info@gotohungary.com

Web Site: http://www.hungary.com/

Iceland

Scandinavian National Tourist Offices

655 Third Ave

New York, NY 10017

(212) 885-9700

Web Site: http://www.goiceland.com

India

India Tourist Office

30 Rockefeller Plaza, North Mezzanine

New York, NY 10112

1-800-953-9399

FAX: (212) 582-3274

Web Site: http://www.tourindia.com

India Tourist Office

3550 Wilshire Blvd #204

Los Angeles, CA 90010

(213) 380-8855

FAX: (213) 380-6111

Web Site: http://www.tourindia.com

Indonesia

Indonesia Tourist Promotion Office

3457 Wilshire Blvd #104

Los Angeles, CA 90010

(213) 387-8309, (213) 387-2078

FAX: (213) 380-4876

Ireland

Irish Tourist Board

345 Park Ave

New York, NY 10154

(800) SHAMROCK, (800) 223-6470

(212) 418-0800

FAX: (212) 371-9052

Email: Contact through the Web site

Web Site: http://www.ireland.travel.ie/

Israel

Israel Government Tourist Info Center

800 Second Avenue

New York, NY 10017

(800) 596-1199, (212) 560-0650

FAX: (212) 499-5645

E-MAIL: hgolan@imot.org

Web Site: http://www.infotour.co.il

Israel Government Tourist Office

6380 Wilshire Blvd #1700

Los Angeles, CA 90048

(800) 596-1199, (213) 658-7462

FAX: (213) 658-6543

Web Site: http://www.infotour.co.il

Italy

Rockefeller Center

630 Fifth Ave

New York, NY 10111

212-245-4822 5618

FAX: (212) 586-9249

Web Site: http://www.italiantourism.com

500 North Michigan Ave

Chicago, IL 60611

(312) 644-0996

FAX: (312) 644-3019

Italian Government Tourist Board

12400 Wilshire Blvd #550

Los Angeles, CA 90025

(310) 820-1898

FAX: (310) 820-6537

Jamaica

Jamaica Tourist Board

3440 Wilshire Blvd, Suite 1207

Los Angeles, CA 90010

(800) 233-4582, (213) 384-1123

FAX: (213) 384-1780

Web Site: http://www.jamaicatravel.com/jtboffice.html

Japan

Japan National Tourist Organization

1 Rockefeller Plaza Ste. 1250

New York, NY 10020

(212) 757-5640

FAX: (212) 307-6754

E-MAIL: jntonyc@interport.net

Web Site: http://www.jnto.go.jp

Japan National Tourist Organization

360 Post Street Suite 601

San Francisco, CA 94108

(415) 989-7140

FAX: (415) 398-5461

E-MAIL: sfjnto@msn.com

Web Site: http://www.jnto.go.jp

Kenya

Kenya Consulate & Tourist Office

424 Madison Ave

New York, NY 10017

(212) 486-1300

FAX: (212) 688-0911

Email: kenya2day@aol.com

Web Site: http://www.embassyofkenya.com

Kenya Consulate & Tourist Office

9150 Wilshire Blvd #160

Beverly Hills, CA 90212

(310) 274-6635

FAX: (310) 859-7010

Web Site: http://www.embassyofkenya.com

Korea

Korea National Tourism Office

1 Executive Drive 7th Floor

Fort Lee, NJ 07024

(201)585-0909

FAX: (201) 585-9041

Web Site: http://www.knto.or.kr

Korea National Tourism Corporation

3435 Wilshire Blvd #350

Los Angeles, CA 90010

(213) 382-3435

FAX: (213) 480-0483

Web Site: http://www.knto.or.kr

Luxembourg

Luxembourg National Tourist Office

17 Beekman Place

New York, NY 10022

(212) 935-8888

FAX: (212) 935-5896

E-MAIL: luxnto@aol.com

Web Site: http://www.visitluxembourg.com/wlcm_mn.htm

Macau

Macau Tourist Information Bureau

3133 Lake Hollywood Dr

Los Angeles, CA 90078

(213) 851-3402

FAX: (213) 851-3684

Malaysia

Tourism Malaysia

120 East 56th St., Suite 810

New York, NY 10022

(212) 754-1113

(800) KLUMPUR

Fax :(212) 754-1116

E-mail : mtpb@aol.com

Web Site : http://www.tourismmalaysia.gov.my

Portal : http://www.malaysiamydestination.com

Tourism Malaysia

818 W Seventh St.,

Los Angeles, CA 90017

(213) 689-9702

Fax : (213) 689-1530

E-mail : malaysiainfo@aol.com

Web Site : http://www.tourismmalaysia.gov.my

Portal : http://www.malaysiamydestination.com

Malta

Malta National Tourist Organization

350 Fifth Avenue Ste. 4412

New York, NY 10118

(212) 695-2233

FAX: (212) 695-8229

E-MAIL: 104452,2005@compuserve.com

Web Site: http://www.visitmalta.com/

Martinique

Martinique Promotion Bureau

A division of the French Government Tourist Office

444 Madison Ave

New York NY 10022

(212) 838-7800

Martinique@NYO.COM

Web Site: http//www.martinique.org

Mexico

Mexico Government Tourist Office

405 Park Ave Ste. 1401

New York, NY 10022

(800) 446-3942

Web Site: http://www.visitmexico.com

Mexico Government Tourist Office

10100 Santa Monica Blvd #224

Los Angeles, CA 90067

(800) 446-3942

Web Site: http://www.visitmexico.com

Monaco

Monaco Government Tourist & Convention Bureau

565 Fifth Ave

New York, NY 10022

(800) 753-9696

E-MAIL: mgto@monaco1.com

Web Site: http://www.monaco.mc/usa

Morocco
Moroccan Tourist Office
20 East 46th St #1201
New York, NY 10017
(212) 557-2520
FAX: (212) 949-8148
Web Site: http://www.tourism-in-morocco.com/

Netherlands
NBT New York
355 Lexington Avenue
New York, NY 10017
(212) 557-3500
FAX: (212) 370-9507
Web Site: http://www.holland.com
E-mail: info@goholland.com

New Zealand
New Zealand Tourism Board
501 Santa Monica Blvd #300
Santa Monica, CA 90401
(800) 388-5494, (310) 395-7480
FAX: (310) 395-5453
Web Site: http://www.purenz.com/

Norway
Norwegian Tourist Board
655 Third Avenue
New York, NY 10017
(212) 885-9700
FAX: (212) 983-5260
Web Site: http://www.norway.org/

Panama

IPAT (The Panama Tourist Bureau)

P.O. Box 4421

Zone 5

The Republic of Panama

Telephone: +507 226-7000 or +507 226-3544

Fax: +507 226-3483 or +507 226-6856

Web Site: http://www.ipat.gob.pa/

Philippines

Philippine Department of Tourism

447 Sutter St #507

San Francisco, CA 94108

(415) 956-4060

FAX: (415) 956-2093

E-MAIL: pdotsf@aol.com

Web Site: http://www.tourism.gov.ph/

Poland

Polish National Tourist Office

275 Madison Ave #1711

New York, NY 10016

(212) 338-9412

FAX: (212) 338-9283

E-MAIL: poltrvl@poland.net

Web Site: www.polandtour.org

Portugal

Portuguese National Tourist Office

590 Fifth Ave

New York, NY 10036

(800) PORTUGAL

Web Site: www.portugal-insite.pt

Puerto Rico
Puerto Rican Tourism Company
575 Fifth Ave 23rd Floor
New York, NY 10017
(212) 599-6262
FAX: (212) 818-1866
Web Site: http://www.prhta.org/

Puerto Rico Tourism Company
P.O. Box 5268
Miami, FL 33102
(800) 866-STAR ext 17
Web Site: http://www.prhta.org/

Puerto Rico Tourism Company
3575 West Cahuenga Blvd, Suite 405
Los Angeles, CA 90068
(800) 874-1230
FAX: (874-7257
Web Site: http://www.prhta.org/

Romania
Romanian Tourist Office
14 East 38th Street, 12th Floor
New York, NY 10016
(212) 545-8484
FAX: (212) 251-0429
Email: onto@erols.com

Russia
The Russian National Tourist Office
130 West 42nd St., Suite 412
New York, NY 10022
(212) 758-1162
FAX: (212) 575-3434
Web Site: http://www.russia-travel.com

Saba & St. Eustatius
Saba & St. Eustatius Tourist Office
c/o Medhurst & Associates, Inc.
271 Main St
Northport, NY 11768
(800) 722-2394

St. Barts
(See French Government Tourist Information)

St. Croix
(See U.S. Virgin Islands)

St. John
(See U.S. Virgin Islands)

St. Kitts & Nevis
St. Kitts & Nevis Tourism Office
414 E. 75th St, 5th Floor
New York, NY 10021
(800) 582-6208
FAX: (212) 734-6511
E-MAIL: skbnev@ix.netcom.com
Web Site: http://www.interknowledge.com/stkitts-nevis

St. Lucia

St. Lucia Tourist Board

820 Second Ave

New York, NY 10017

(800) 456-3984, (212) 867-2950

FAX: (212) 867-2795

Web Site: http://www.st-lucia.com/

St. Marten

Sint Maarten Tourism Office

675 Third Avenue Ste. 1806

New York, NY 10017

(800) 786-2278, (212) 953-2084

FAX: (212) 953-2145

Web Site: http://www.st-maarten.com

St. Thomas

(See U.S. Virgin Islands)

St. Vincent & The Grenadines

St. Vincent & the Grenadines Tourist Office

801 Second Ave, 21st Floor

New York, NY 10017

(800) 729-1726

FAX: (212) 949-5946

Web Site: http://www.stvincentandgrenadines.com

Scandinavia (Iceland, Norway, Sweden, Denmark, Finland)
Scandinavian National Tourist Offices
655 Third Ave
New York, NY 10017
(212) 885-9700
FAX: (212) 983-5260
Web Site: http://www.goscandinavia.com

Scotland
(See Great Britain)

Singapore
Singapore Tourist Promotion Board
590 Fifth Ave 12th Floor
New York, NY 10036
(212) 302-4861
FAX: (212) 302-4801
Web Site: www.singapore-usa.com

Singapore Tourist Promotion Board
8484 Wilshire Blvd #510
Beverly Hills, CA 90211
(323) 852-1901
Web Site: www.singapore-usa.com

Saint Maarten
Saint Maarten Tourism Office
675 Third Avenue Ste. 1806
New York, NY 10017
(800) 786-2278, (212) 953-2084
FAX: (212) 953-2145
Web Site: http://www.st-maarten.com

Slovenia
Slovenia Tourist Office
345 E. 12th St.
New York, NY 10003
(212) 358-9686
FAX: (212) 358-9025
Email: slotouristboard@sloveniatravel.com
Web site: www.slovenia-tourism.si

Spain
Tourist Office of Spain
666 Fifth Ave 35th Floor
New York, NY 10022
1-888-OKSPAIN
(212) 265-8822
FAX: (212) 265-8864
Web Site http://www.okspain.org

Tourist Office of Spain
8383 Wilshire Blvd #960
Beverly Hills, CA 90211
(213) 658-7188
FAX: (213) 658-1061
Web Site http://www.okspain.org

Sweden
Scandinavian Tourist Board
655 Third Avenue
New York, NY 10017
(212) 885-9700
FAX: (212) 983-5260
Web Site: http://www.gosweden.org/

Switzerland
Switzerland Tourism
608 Fifth Ave
New York, NY 10020
(212) 757-5944
FAX: (212) 262-6116
Web Site: http://www.switzerlandtourism.ch/

Switzerland Tourism
150 N Michigan Avenue, Suite 2930
Chicago, IL 60601
(312) 332-9900
FAX: (312) 630-5848
Web Site: http://www.switzerlandtourism.ch/

Switzerland Tourism
222 N Sepulveda Blvd #1570
El Segundo, CA 90245
(310) 640-8900
FAX: (310) 335 5982
Web Site: http://www.switzerlandtourism.ch/

Syria
Tourist Office of Syria
c/o Syrian Consulate
2215 Wyoming Ave, Northwest DC, 20008
(202) 232-6313
FAX: (202) 265-4585
Web site: www.syriatourism.org

Tahiti

Tahiti Tourist Promotion Board

300 N Continental Blvd #180

El Segundo, CA 90245

(800) 365-4949 (to order brochures only)

(310) 414-8484

FAX: (310) 414-8490

Web Site: http://www.tahiti-tourisme.com

Taiwan

Taiwan Visitors Association

405 Lexington Avenue, 37th Floor

New York, NY 10174

(212) 466-0691

FAX: (212) 432-6436

Web Site: http://www.tbroc.gov.tw

Taiwan Visitors Association

333 N Michigan Ave

Chicago, IL 60601

(312) 346-1038

FAX: (312) 346-1037

Web Site: http://www.tbroc.gov.tw

Taiwan Visitors Association

166 Geary St #1605

San Francisco, CA 94108

(415) 989-8677

FAX: (415) 989-7242

Web Site: http://www.tbroc.gov.tw

Thailand

Thailand Tourist Authority

1 World Trade Center Suite 3729

New York, NY 10048

(212) 432-0433

FAX: (212) 912-0920

E-MAIL: tatny@aol.com

Thailand Tourist Authority

3440 Wilshire Blvd #1100

Los Angeles, CA 90010

(213) 461-9814

FAX: (213) 461-9834

E-MAIL: tatla@ix.netcom.com

Tonga

Tonga Consulate General

360 Post St #604

San Francisco, CA 94108

(415) 781-0365

FAX: (415) 781-3964

Trinidad & Tobago

Trinidad & Tobago Tourism Development Authority

7000 Boulevard East

Guttenberg, NJ 07093

(800) 748-4224

FAX: (201) 869-7628

Web Site: http://www.visittnt.com/

Turkey
Turkish Tourism & Information Office
821 United Nations Plaza
New York, NY 10017
(212) 687-2194
E-MAIL: tourney@soho.ios.com
Web Site: http://www.turkey.org/turkey

Turks & Caicos
Turks & Caicos Tourist Board
P. O. Box 128
Grand Turk
Turks & Caicos, BWI
(800) 241-0824
FAX: (809) 946-2733
Web Site: http://www.turksandcaicostourism.com/

US Virgin Islands (St. Croix, St. John, St. Thomas)
U.S. Virgin Islands Division of Tourism
1270 Avenue of the Americas #2108
New York, NY 10020
(212) 332-2222
FAX: (212) 332-2223
Web Site: http://www.usvi.net

U.S. Virgin Islands Division of Tourism
3460 Wilshire Blvd #412
Los Angeles, CA 90010
(213) 739-0138
FAX: (213) 739-2096
Web Site: http://www.usvi.net

Wales
(See Great Britain)

Glossary Of Travel Terms

(Learn to understand Travel & Toursim)

Accommodations: rooms in hotel, motel B&B.

Adjoining rooms: Two rooms located next to each other, usually with no door connecting them.

Adventure tour: A tour designed around an adventurous activity such as rafting, hiking, or mountain climbing.

Affinity group: A group of people that share a common hobby, interest, or activity, or that are united through regular participation in shared outings. Also see preformed group

After-departure charge: Charges that do not appear on the guest's bill at check out such as telephone or dining charges.

Agent: One who has the power to act at the representative of another. Most frequently in travel, a specific kind of agent such as a travel agent.

AIO variables: Activities, interests, and opinions-used to measure and categorize customer lifestyles.

Air sea: A cruises or travel package in which one or more transportation elements are provided by air and one or more by sea. The package is usually combined with local lodging.

Airline fare: Price charged for an airline ticket. Several types of fares exist and can change with market conditions.

Airlines Reporting Corporation (ARC): An organization that provides a method of approving authorized agency locations for the sale of transportation and cost-effective procedures for processing records and funds of such sales to carrier customers.

All-inclusive package: A tour package in which most travel elements are purchased for set price. Also called an all-expense package.

Alumni tour: A tour created for customers who have previously traveled with a tour operator. Also called a reunion tour.

Amenity package: A cluster of special features, such as complimentary shore excursions, bar or boutique credit, or wine at dinner offered to clients on a given tour or cruise, usually as a bonus or extra feature. Usually used to induce clients to book through a particular travel agency or organization.

Attractions: An item or specific interest to travelers, such as natural wonders, manmade facilities and structures, entertainment, and activities.

Average room rate: The total guest room revenue for a given period divided by the number of rooms occupied for the same period.

Back to back: A term used to describe tours operating on a consistent, continuing basis. For instance, a motor coach arriving in a city from a cross-country tour may conclude the first tour upon arrival, and then transport a second group back along the same route to the origination city of the first tour.

Baggage handler: See porter

Baggage master: The person who controls baggage handling on a ship.

Bed and breakfast (B&B): Overnight accommodations usually in a private home or boarding house, often with a full American-style or Continental breakfast included in one rate.

Bell captain: The person in charge of luggage at a hotel.

Block: A number of rooms, seats, or space reserved in advance, usually by wholesalers, tour operators, or receptive operators who intend to sell them as components of tour packages.

Boarding pass: The document that allows a traveler to pass through the gate area and onto a plane or ship.

Booking form: A document which purchasers of tours must complete to give the operator full particulars about who is buying the tour. It states exactly what is being purchased (including options) and must be signed as acknowledgment that the liability clause has been read and understood.

Breakage: Expenses budgeted for a tour but not used or expended, thus resulting in additional profit to the tour operator. Examples include meals budgeted but not consumed, currency fluctuations in favor of the tour operator, or the tour selling too much larger numbers of passengers than expected.

Break-even point (BEP): The point at which revenues and expenses are the same. For example, the BEP is the number of products (or seats, cabins, tickets, etc.) that must be sold for a company to break even. The BEP is calculated as fixed costs divided by the selling price less variable costs. See reasonable number

Break-even pricing: Pricing a product based on a forecast of the break-even point and the cost of achieving the break-even point.

Budgeted balance sheet: A budget that measures total assets and liabilities.

Budgeted income statement: A budget that tracks revenues and expenses. Also called the profit and loss statement.

Cabin: A sleeping room on a ship.

Carrier: A company that provides transportation services, such as motor coach companies, airlines, cruise lines, and rental car agencies.

Cash flow: Monies available to meet a company's daily operating expenses, as opposed to equity, accounts receivable, or other credits not immediately accessible.

Cash budget: A budget that monitors cash flow and funds available to meet current expenses.

Casual research: A form of marketing research that is used to test cause-and-effect relationships between a marketing program and customers.

Certified Tour Professional (CTP): A designation conferred upon tour professionals who have completed a prescribed course of academic study, professional service, tour employment, and evaluation requirements. The CTP program is administered by the

National Tour Association (Lexington, KY) and is open to individuals employed in any segment of the tourism industry.

Certified Travel Counselor (CTC): A designation attesting to professional competence as a travel agent. It is conferred upon travel professionals with five or more years of industry experience who compete a two-year graduate-level travel management program administered by the Institute of Certified Travel Agents (Wellesley, MA).

Certified Travel Industry Specialist (CTIS): A designation conferred upon American Bus Association member company employees who successfully complete five correspondence courses (three) required and two electives and written evaluation of eight marketplace seminars.

Chain-ratio method: A method for forecasting market demand by multiplying a base market figure by a series of consumption constraints.

Chamber of Commerce: A DMO that operates at the local level and is comprised of businesses that are not necessarily associated with the tourism industry.

Charter: To hire the exclusive use of any aircraft, motor coach, or other vehicle.

Charter service: The transportation of preformed groups (organized by someone other than the carrier), which have the exclusive use of the vehicle.

Circle itinerary: A travel routing design that overnights in different locations and returns to the point of departure without retracing the travel route.

City guide: A tour guide who points out and comments on the highlights of a city, usually from a motor coach or van.

City tour: A sightseeing trip through a city, usually lasting a half-day or a full day, during which a guide points out the city's highlights.

Client list: A printout of the names of all tour participants.

Client mix: Objectives set by companies to achieve percentages of customers from different market segments.

Closed-end question: A question for which the answers are provided for the respondent, who chooses only from those answers.

Closeout: Finalization of a tour, cruise, or similar group travel project after which time no further clients are accepted. Any unsold air or hotel space is released, and final lists and payments are sent to all suppliers.

Commission: A percentage of a travel product's price that is returned to the distributor when the product is sold.

Commissionable tour: A tour available through retail and wholesale travel agencies, which provides for a payment of an agreed-upon sales commission to the retailer or wholesale seller.

Common carrier: Any person or organization that offers transportation for a fee.

Comp policy: Arrangements for free tickets, rooms, meals, etc.

Complimentary (comps): Items provided free of charge, such as rooms, meals, tickets, airfare, gifts, souvenirs, etc.

Computerized reservation system (CRS): An automated system used by travel agents that contains pricing, availability and product descriptions for hotels, car rentals, cruises, and air transportation.

Conditions: The section or clause of a transportation or tour contract that specifies what is not offered and that may spell out the circumstances under which the contract may be invalidated (in whole or in part).

Configuration: The interior arrangement of a vehicle, particularly an airplane. The same airplane, for example, may be configured for 190 coach-class passengers, or it may hold 12 first-class passengers and 170 coach passengers, or any other combination within its capacity.

Confirmed reservation: An oral or written statement by a supplier that he has received and will honor a reservation. Oral confirmations have virtually no legal weight. Even written or faxed confirmations have specified or implied limitations. For example, a hotel is usually not obliged to honor a reservation if a guest arrives after 6 p.m., unless late arrival has been guaranteed.

Connecting flight: A flight that requires a passenger to change planes as part of the itinerary.

Connecting room: Two rooms that are connected to each other by a door.

Consolidator: A person or company that forms groups to travel on air charters at group rates on scheduled flights to increase sales, earn override commissions, or reduce the possibility of tour cancellations.

Consolidation: Cancellation by a charter tour operator of one more flights associated with a specific charter departure or departure period, with the transfer of passengers to another charter flight or flights to depart on or near the same day. Also, selling the same tour with identical departure dates through a number of wholesalers, cooperatives, or other outlets in order to increase sales and reduce the possibility of tour cancellations.

Consortium: A collection of organizations made up of independently owned and managed agencies that band together to increase their buying power.

Consumer protection plan: A plan offered by a company and/or association that protects the customer's deposits and payments from loss in the event of company bankruptcy.

Consumer: The actual user of a product or service. See also customer

Consumption constraints: Issues that limit the number of people in a market who will purchase a product.

Continental breakfast: At a minimum, a beverage (coffee, tea, or milk) and rolls and toast, with fruit juice sometimes included.

Contract: A legally enforceable agreement between two or more parties.

Convenience sample: A collection of research subjects who are the easiest for the researcher to select.

Convention and Visitors Bureau (CVB): A nonprofit DMO that operates at the county and city level. A CVB typically encourages groups to hold meetings, conventions, and trade shows in its city.

Cooperative (co-op) advertising: An agreement between two parties to share the cost of placing an advertisement.

Co-op tour: Selling a tour through a number of wholesalers, cooperatives, or other outlets in order to increase sales and reduce the possibility of tour cancellations.

Costing: The process of itemizing and calculating all the costs the tour operator will pay on a given tour.

Cost-plus pricing: See markup pricing

Coupon: See voucher

Custom tour: A travel package created specifically for a preformed group or niche market.
 Customer: The buyer of a product or service. See consumer

Customs: The common term for U.S. Customs Service, the federal agency charged with collecting duty on specified items imported into the country. The agency also restricts the entry of forbidden items.

Database: A computerized, organized collection of individual customer information.

Day rate: Also called a day room. A reduced rate granted for the use of a guest room during the daytime, not overnight occupancy. Usually provided on a tour when a very late-night departure is scheduled.

Day tour: An escorted or unescorted tour that lasts less than 24 hours and usually departs and returns on the same day. See sightseeing tour

Deadheading: Making a trip or a segment of a trip without passengers, such as driving an empty motor coach somewhere.

Demand generators: Strategies and programs developed by DMOs and suppliers to generate destination demand. Examples include festivals, events, cultural tours, and consumer promotion.

Demands: A consumer's wants backed by the ability to purchase.

Demographics: Population measures, such as age, gender, income, education, race/ethnicity, religion, marital status, household size, and occupation.

Departure point: The location or destination from which a tour officially begins.

Departure tax: Fee collected from a traveler by the host country at the time of departure.

Deposit: An advance payment required to obtain and confirm space.

Deposit policy: A specified amount or a percentage of the total bill due on a specified date prior to arrival.

Descriptive research: a form of marketing research that is used to provide detailed answers about customer markets.

Destination: The geographic place to which a traveler is going.

Destination alliance: A DMO that operates as a for-profit association of select suppliers who form a paid-membership network to promote their services to travelers.

Destination management company (DMC): A for-profit company that operates similar to a CVB by providing planning and execution services for the convention and meeting market.

Destination marketing organization (DMO): An organization that promotes a location (city, region, state province, country) as a travel destination.

Direct flight: A flight that stops one or more times on the way to a destination, but does not require travelers to change planes.

Direct marketing: Sales and marketing communication that feature direct interaction between a company and its customers without any distribution intermediaries.

Double double: A room with two double beds.

Double-occupancy rate: The price per person for a room to be shared with another person; the rate most frequently quoted in tour brochures.

Double-room rate: The full price of a room for two people (twice the double-occupancy rate.)

Docent: A tour guide who works free of charge at a museum.

Downgrade: To move to a lesser level of accommodations or a lower class of service.

Driver-guide: A tour guide who does double duty by driving a vehicle while narrating.

Duty-free imports: Item amounts and categories specified by a government that are fee of tax or duty charges when brought into the country.

Economic impact study: Research into the dollars generated by an industry and how these dollars impact the economy through direct spending and the indirect impact of additional job creation and the generation of income and tax revenue.

Eco-tour: A tour designed to focus on preserving the environment, or a tour traveling to environmentally sensitive areas.

Educational tour: A tour designed around an educational activity, such as studying art.

Environmental scanning: The process of monitoring important forces in the business environment for trends and changes that may impact a company.

Errors and Omissions Insurance: Insurance coverage equivalent to malpractice insurance, protecting an agent or operator's staff if an act of negligence, an error, or an omission occurs that causes a client great hardship or expense.

Escort: See tour director

Escorted group tour: A group tour that features a tour director who travels with the group throughout the trip to provide sightseeing commentary and coordinate all group movement and activities.

Escrow accounts: Funds placed in the custody of licensed financial institutions for safekeeping. Many contracts in travel require that agents and tour operators maintain customers' deposits and prepayments in escrow accounts.

Exchange order: See voucher

Exploratory research: A form of marketing research that's used to obtain preliminary information and clues. It is most often used when the marketing problem is ambiguous.

Extension: A fully arranged sub-tour offered optionally at extra cost to buyers of a tour or cruise. Extensions may occur before, during, or after the basic travel program.

FAM (familiarization) tour: A free or reduced-rate trip offered to travel professionals to acquaint them with what a destination, attraction, or supplier has to offer.

Fixed costs: Costs that don't change with sales or production levels.

Fly/drive tour: An F.I.T. package that always includes air travel and a rental car and sometimes other travel components.

Folio: An itemized record of a guest's charges and credits, which is maintained in the front office until departure. Also referred to as a guest bill or guest statement.

Frequent Independent travel (F.I.T.): A custom-designed, prepaid travel package with many individualized arrangements. F.I.T. are unescorted and usually have no formal itinerary.

Full house: A hotel with all guest rooms occupied.

Function room: A special room that is used primarily for private parties, banquets, and meetings. Also called banquet rooms.

Gateway: City, airport, or area from which a flight or tour departs.

Gateway city: City with an international airport.

Ground operator: See receptive operator

Group leader: An individual who has been given the responsibility of coordinating tour and travel arrangements for a group. The group leader may act as a liaison to a tour operator or may develop a tour independently (and sometimes serve as the tour director).

Group rate: A special discounted rate charged by suppliers to groups. Also called tour rate.

Group tour: A travel package for an assembly of travelers that has a common itinerary, travel date, and transportation. Group tours are usually prearranged, prepaid, and include transportation, lodging, dining, and attraction admissions. See also escorted group tour

Guaranteed tour: A tour guaranteed to operate unless canceled before an established cutoff date (usually 60 days prior to departure).

Guest account: See folio

Guide or guide service: A person or company qualified to conduct tours of specific localities or attractions.

Guided tour: A local sightseeing trip conducted by a guide.

Head tax: Fee charged for arriving and departing passengers in some foreign countries.

High season: See peak season

Hosted group tour: A group tour that features a representative (the host) of the tour operator, destination, or other tour provider, who interacts with the group only for a few hours a day to provide information and arrange for transportation. The host usually does not accompany the group as it travels.

House: A synonym used for hotel.

Hub-and-spoke itinerary: A travel routing design that uses a central destination as the departure and return point for day trips to outlying destinations and attractions.

Inbound operator: A receptive operator that usually serves groups arriving from another country.

Inbound tour: A tour for groups of travelers whose trip originates in another location, usually another country.

Incentive or incentive commission: See override

Incentive tour: A trip offered as a prize, particularly to stimulate the productivity of employees or sales agents.

Incidentals: Charges incurred by the participants of a tour, but which are not included in the tour price.

Inclusive tour: See all-inclusive package

Independent tour: A travel package in which a tour operator is involved only with the planning, marketing, and selling of the package, but is not involved with the passengers while the tour is in progress. See also frequent independent travel (F.I.T.)

Interlobular tour: A tour that uses several forms of transportation, such as a plane, motor coach, cruise ship, and train.

Involvement device: An element of direct mail that gets the reader involved in the process of evaluating and/or responding to the solicitation.

Itinerary: A list of a tour's schedule and major travel elements.

Judgment sample: A sample based on the researcher's choice of subjects for a study.

Land operator: See receptive operator

Leg: Portion of a journey between two scheduled stops.

Letter of agreement: A letter from the buyer to the supplier accepting the terms of the proposal. This may also be the supplier's first proposal that has been initialed by the buyer.

List broker: A seller of mail lists for direct marketing.

Load factor: The number of passengers traveling on a vehicle, vessel, or aircraft compared to the number of available seats or cabins.

Locator map: A map of an area or a city, showing locations of attractions and hotels.

Lodging: Any establishment that provides shelter and overnight accommodations to travelers.

Logistics: Management of the details of an operation.

Low season: See off peak

Microenvironment: The broad forces in society and the business world that impact most companies.

Management company: A firm that owns several lodging properties.

Manifest: Final official listing of all passengers and/or cargo aboard a transportation vehicle or vessel.

Market demand: The amount of a specific product or service that may be purchased during a certain period of time in a particular geographic area.

Market forecast: The realistic demand within a given time period for the products produced by all companies within a certain industry or product category.

Market segmentation: The process of dividing a broad market into smaller, specific markets based on customer characteristics, buying power, and other variables.

Market share: The measure of company sales versus total sales for a specific product category or industry.

Market: All existing and potential customers for a product or service.

Marketing mix: The 4 Ps of marketing: product, price, promotion, place (distribution).

Marketing plan: A written report that details marketing objectives for a product or service, and recommends strategies for achieving these objectives.

Marketing research: The function that links the consumer, customer, and public to the marketer through the systematic gathering and analyzing of information.

Markup pricing: Pricing a product by adding a standard markup to costs. Also called cost-plus pricing

Markup: A percentage added to the cost of a product to achieve a selling price.

Master account: The guest account for a particular group or function that will be paid by the sponsoring organization. See folio

Media: Communications channel such as broadcast (radio, TV), print (newspapers, magazines, direct mail), outdoor (billboards), and multimedia (Internet).

Meet-and-greet service: A pre-purchased service for meeting and greeting clients upon arrival in a city, usually at the airport, pier, or rail station, and assisting clients with entrance formalities, collecting baggage, and obtaining transportation.

Meeting/conference tour: A tour designed around a specific meeting or conference for the participants.

Microenvironment: Those forces close to a company that impact operations and marketing programs.

Mission statement: The concise description of what an organization is, its purpose, and what it intends to accomplish.

Motor coach tour: A tour that features the motor coach the form of transportation to and from destinations.

Motor coach tour operators: Tour operators that own their own motor coaches.

Motor coach: A large, comfortable bus that can transport travelers and their luggage long distances.

Multi-day tour: A travel package of two or more days. Most multi-day tours are escorted, all-inclusive packages.

Murder-mystery tour: A tour that features a staged "murder" and involves travelers in solving the crime.

Mystery tour: A journey to unpublicized destinations in which tour takers aren't told where they will be going until en route or upon arrival.

National tourism organization (NTO): A federal-government-level DMO that promotes country as a travel destination.

Needs: Those aspects of the life a person can't do without.

Net wholesale rate: A rate usually slightly lower than the wholesale rate, applicable to groups of individuals when a hotel is specifically mentioned in a tour brochure. The rate is marked up by wholesale sellers of tours to cover distribution and promotion costs.

Niche market: A highly specialized segment of the travel market, such as an affinity group with a unique special interest.

No show: A guest with confirmed reservations who does not arrive and whose reservation was not canceled.

Objective and task method: A process for creating a promotion budget that sets objectives first, then defines the tasks needed to achieve those objectives, and then commits funds necessary to perform the tasks.

Occupancy: The percentage of available rooms occupied for a given period. It is computed by dividing the number of rooms occupied for a period by the number of rooms available for the same period.

Off peak: Slow booking periods for suppliers. Also called the low season.

On-site guide: A tour guide who conducts tours of one or several hours' duration at a specific building, attraction, or site.

Open-ended question: A question that allows the respondent to provide a free-response answer.

Open-jaw itinerary: A travel routing design that departs from one location and returns to another. For example, travelers may fly into one city and depart from another one. Or a traveler may purchase round-trip transportation from the point of origin to one destination, at which another form of transportation is used to reach a second destination, where the traveler resumes the initial form of transportation to return to the point of origin.

Operations: Performing the practical work of operating a tour or travel program.

Operator: See Tour Operator

Optionals: Optional tour features that are not included in the base tour price, such as sightseeing excursions or special activities.

Outbound operator: A company that takes groups from a given city or country to another city or country.

Outbound tour: A tour that takes travelers out of the area, usually from a domestic city to another country.

Overbook: Accepting reservations for more space than is available.

Overhead: Those fixed costs involved in regular operations, such as rent, insurance, management salaries, and utilities.

Override: A commission over and above the normal base commission percentage.

Packaged travel: A package in combination of two or more types of tour components into a product, which is produced, assembled, promoted and sold as a package by a tour operator for an all-inclusive price.

Passenger vessel: Ships, yachts, ferries, boats, etc.

Patronage Program: A program that rewards the customer for loyalty and repeat purchase, such as frequent-flyer programs.

Peak season: A destination's high season when demand is strong. Also called the high season.

Per capita costs: Per-person costs.

Per capita tour: See scheduled tour

Perceived value: The ratio of perceived benefits to perceived price.

Port of entry: Destination providing customs and immigration services.

Porter: A person who handles luggage at an airport, train station, etc.; also called skycap or baggage handler.

The GEM Group Consulting Services

We are here to help you succeed!

Need Help?

Contact the author "Gerry" Mitchell

The GEM Group is now offering "Direct Contact and Consulting Services" with the author and founder of The GEM Tour Guide System.[©] Gerald Mitchell furnishes solid consulting with refreshing informality. Gerald enriches his advice with his own experience as a tour guide, lecturer, educator and consultant to clients from around the world. With contagious enthusiasm, you will be guided by Gerald's Consulting Services with Gerald Mitchell, founder of Tour Guides USA ©

Tour Guiding, like all enterprises, is likely to benefit you in proportion to your investment in it. If in addition to a fair profit and the professional tour guides' pride, you can reap from it the satisfaction of having done a professional service to your clients, you will experience the magical glow prized by those for whom tour guiding has become a unique joy and life's vocation.   Good Guiding!

How The Gem Group Ltd. Can Help You

✓ What is your purpose for purchasing this book?

✓ What are your Objectives?

✓ What are your interest/Hobbies?

✓ What are your strengths?

Do You Require Assistance On The Following Subjects?

- Sales, Marketing & Promotional Assistance
- Tour Designing
- Guide Training
- Brochure Development
- Advertising
- Web Site Design
- Upcoming Training Workshops
- Other

If the GEM Group can assist you in starting your own tour guide business, please complete the form on the following page and e-mail –gem39@bellsouth.net t to the attention of Gerry Mitchell.

Confidential Client Profile- Consulting Service Form

Name: _____

Address: (Residence)_____

_____

_____

Phone:_____ E-mail:_____

URL:_____

Present Occupation:_____ Title:_____

Company:_____

Formal Education:_____

Hospitality – Tourism experience (s):

_____

_____

_____

_____

List your goals Objectives and Comments:

_____

_____

_____

_____

_____

_____

_____

_____

_____

_____

_____

How can The GEM Group HELP YOU develop Tour Guide Company?

#1_____

_____

_____

_____

#2_____

_____

_____

_____

#3_____

_____

_____

_____

#4_____

_____

_____

_____

#5_____

_____

_____

_____

TAKE OFF!

&

Learn How to Start a Tour Guiding Business
Turn your talents in Profits
Leave Corporate Stress Behind, be your own Boss
Learn how this book can benefit you and your fututure

Learn how to start a Tour Guiding Business from a *30 year veteran*. This comprehensive manual takes you in detail through **eight steps** to starting a Tour Guiding Business. Tour Guides serve as a source of answers to questions covering local history, flora, fishing, golf, wildlife and where best to dine.

g.e Mitchell
Author, Tour Designer & Lecturer   Gerry Mitchell has conducted seminars from the Amazon to the Canadian Arctic. Mitchell's works are currently in use in the United States, the Middle East, Caribbean Basin, Canada, Latin America, and Russia. Registered with Who's Who.*Organizations of American States (OAS) *World Bank—*US Commerce Department, *United States Agency International Development (USAid)

The GEM Group Est. 1976 -To order: www.tour-guiding.com. ©How to Start a Tour Guiding Business,2005, All rights reserved.-Library of Congress   ISBN 0-946439-10-5 USA-Made in USA

TAKE OFF!

For

A career in the Travel-Tourism Industry

➤ Get packed for life-enhancing experiences of a lifetime!
➤ Let a 25 year expert be your guide helping you map out a exciting career in the Global Travel-Tourism industry
➤ Learn "Inside Secrets" to where the high paying jobs are!
➤ Learn how to write a resume for success!
➤ Find career stability and financial satisfaction!

g.e Mitchell
Author, Tour Designer & Lecturer

Gerry Mitchell has conducted seminars from the Amazon to the Canadian Arctic. Mitchell's works are currently in use in the United States, the Middle East, Caribbean Basin, Canada, Latin America, and Russia. Registered with Who's Who.*Organizations of American States (OAS) *World Bank—*US Commerce Department, *United States Agency International Development (USAid)

The GEM Group, Ltd Est. 1976- www.tour-guiding.com. ©Global travel-Tourism Career Opportunities .2005, All rights reserved. Library of Congress ISBN 0-946439-14-8 Made in USA

Workshop & Seminar Testimonials

Over 7,000 participants...150,000 hours of training provided
The GEM Group takes your there...we push your vision to the limits!

"Gerald E. Mitchell is one of the best speakers I have heard. He keeps the class interested and makes learning fun and interesting."
- Dr.Russell Backardt, Western Carolina University

"A dynamic speaker and instructor. Should be used on a continuous basis in our Tourism industry to teach and educate various sectors of the industry on the whole."
- Laurie McConnell, Travel Away Tours

"All I can really say is "thank God" you sponsored this workshop. It is the real program to come along and I know with your caring feeling that there's more to come."
- Justine Clinton, St. Lucia

"This is the first time I have attended a seminar on this topic that has been conducted with so much focus towards achieving real practical objectives."
- Richard Spei, Toronto, Canada

"We wish to express our most sincere appreciation for your tremendous contribution to the Business Management for Women tourism session for the delegates from the former Soviet Union. We are confident that the delegates took home practical information needed to upgrade their tour companies and establish useful future relationships with U.S. companies as a result of the excellent program you provided."
- Liesel Duhon, Director, Sabit United States Depart. Of Commerce, International Trade Adminitration, Washington, D.C.

"Extremely informative, and educational, and I feel that I learned a great deal to apply and hopefully turn these hours into profits."
- Lester Winston, Trinidad West Indies

"Gerald E. Mitchell is one of the best speakers I have heard. He keeps the class interested and makes learning fun."
- Dr. Joe Manjone, University of Alabama, Huntsville

"The Tour Guide manual made it possible for me to start my own business. I read all your books, made notes that I needed to refer to often, highlighted other topics, and then reread the book. It has become a real workbook for my staff. Thank you for helping me gain financial freedom and be my own boss. "
- Maria Jackson, US Army Recreational Services

"The author, Gerry Mitchell, has provided practical advice, and models to follow. This is the best book I've seen on the subject. "
- Aura J. Carter, Hotel Manager, Barbados, West Indies

Join the GEM Group by Starting your own Tour Guiding Service

How to Start a Tour Guide Service Service©
The Workshop

Invest In You!
Invest in Your Personal Growth…

Attend a 5-day comprehensive training workshop
"How to start a Tour Guide Service"©
With an acclaimed 25 Year Veteran of the Travel Service Business

Start NOW by turning your talents into profits!
Lean How To:

- ☒ Design and plan creative Historical & Heritage Walking Tours
- ☒ Evening Dine-Arounds
- ☒ Nightclub Tours
- Special Events Coordinator
- ☒ Golf Outing
- ☒ Fishing Tournaments/Expeditions
- ☒ Soft &High Eco-Adventure Tours
- Hosting Film Crews - from Hollywood and abroad
- ☒ Indigenous Arts and Crafts Seminars and Participatory Workshops
- ☒ Cruise Ship Excursions

What is included in the GEM Institute of Travel-Tourism Global Career Development workshop?

- ☑ **GEM Training manuals and handouts, sample tours and tariffs**
- ☑ **25 hour of instruction by qualified tourism/hospitality professionals**
- ☑ **The 8 easy steps to establishing a successful Tour Guide Service©**
- ☑ **The Welcome and Farewell dinner**
- ☑ **Hotel accommodations**
- ☑ **Hotel taxes and tips**
- ☑ **On-site touring with transportation and professional tour guide instructors**
- ☑ **Your GEM Institute of Travel-tourism Global Career Development certificate**
- ☑ **Professional guest speakers and trainers representing over 10 opportunities within the guiding industry share their knowledge and experiences by offering insider tips and advices on –**

"How to Guide" individuals or groups for:
- ☒ **Historical, Cultural, Walking tours**
- ☒ **Hiking**
- ☒ **Sports**
- ☒ **Fishing**
- ☒ **Kayaking - Boating**
- ☒ **Soft Adventure**
- ☒ **Religious**
- ☒ **Young Adults**
- ☒ **Family Tours & Reunions**
- ☒ **Weddings**
- ☒ **Cruise Lines - Tour Guide Shore Excursions**
- ☒ **Gay and Lesbian Tours**

☑ **Acquire skills for Web Site Design & E-Marketing your Tour Guide Services and Tours**

Essential skills you will learn at the GEM Institute of Travel-Tourism Global Career Development workshop –

Step #1- Introduction to Customer Relations

How to handle reservations for individuals and groups

Step #2- Introduction to the Professional Tour Guide Service

How to deal with problems, conducting walking tours, dealing with difficult questions, creating a positive group dynamic, honing your presentation skills, piecing your commentary together, projecting your voice, knowing your topic.

Step #3 - Preparing an extensive business plan for your Tour Guide Company

Step #4 - Researching & Collecting travel data for your tour services

Learn how to select your tour suppliers, hotels, motor coaches etc.

Step #5 - Designing Creative and Profitable Tours

The workshop shows you how to present a summary of your tour services, highlights of trips, and the unique features your Tour Guide Company has to offer.

Step #6 - Designing Tour Brochures

Step #7 - Guidelines for pricing your tours and services for profit!

The price is usually the key decision factor for the client in purchasing your tours. You will learn how to motivate the target market and leave enough margin to make a profit.

Step #8 - Developing sustainable Marketing Strategies

Learn" Niche" marketing - how to target your tours to a demographic characteristic – segmenting prospects by income and geographic location. Retired? Yuppie? Single? Adventure/Thrill seeker?

Why Charleston, South Carolina?

Charleston has been Ranked the #5th Top City in America to Visit and Tour!

The Good Word About Charleston

"Charleston is still an uncrowded city of human scale, where church steeples remain the highest points. As Emily Whaley says of her garden, 'this is a place to let your soul catch up with you.'" - **Condé Nast Traveler**

"The sound of horse drawn carriages. Mansions dressed up and looking almost bejeweled with their wrought iron terraces and gates. Secret alleys lit by flickering lamps. Charleston may well be the most romantic of cities."
- **National Geographic**

"In my opinion there is nowhere in America which expresses the European appeal as much as Charleston, South Carolina. From the English to the Spanish influence it gives the city the most unique feeling in America." - **Spa Management** (Britain)

Awards and Honors

Ranked the number one safest and culturally most fascinating cities in the US
- **TravelSmart**

One of the World's Best Unspoiled Destinations
- **National Geographic Traveler**

America's most mannerly city for 10th consecutive year
- **Etiquette expert Marjabelle Young Stewart**

8th Top City of the United States & Canada
- **Travel+Leisure**

A Top 10 Art Destination in the USA
- **American Style Magazine**

Center for Women's Travel - Tourism

Since 1976 The GEM Group has provided training for women around the globe in how to start their own business within the Travel &Tourism industry.

Women's Groups: UAW, Women's Association-Surnime, Amazon- Inuit Women Tour Guide/Destination Managers, Canadian Artic (NWT,) -Desk & Derrick,-Activities Coordinator's for the National Parks and Recreation,-US Military- Moral Welfare and Recreation (MWR), Caribbean Basin, Association of Business Owners (Hospitality & Tourism),- her Majesty Queen Noor of Jordan ,National Parks Society Program

Women's Role in the Tourism Industry. Examples of women and women's groups starting their own income generating businesses are plentiful. Increasingly appealing to women, these businesses help to create financial independence for local women and challenge them to develop the necessary skills and support opportunities to increase their education. Research has shown that financial independence and good education lead to improved self-esteem of women and more equitable relationships in families and communities.

Both Women's Rights: The United Nations Convention on the Elimination of all Forms of Discrimination Against Women (CEDAW, 1979), and the Universal Declaration of Human Rights (1948) form the basis of addressing human rights and women's rights issues in the tourism industries. Case studies show that women can find a voice and independence through getting involved in tourism activities by becoming part of decision-making processes and carving out new roles in their families, in their homes and communities, and within local power structures. Source: www.theearthsummit.org 2004

"I would highly recommend the GEM Tour Manuals. The author, Mr. Mitchell, makes sharp analysis of what it takes to bring tour components together for a finished product, a quality tour package. This wonderfully insightful, to-the-point manual will be of great help to travel professionals."
- **Michael Pinchbeck, B.Ed., Executive Director, Bahamas Hotel Training College**

Registration form for the G E M Tour Guide Workshops
You're Personal Data: www .tour-guiding.com

Limited to 20 participants!

Registration Fee: $975.00 (based on double occupancy)
Single rate provided upon request
Payment Schedule: $200.00 initial deposit- Final payment: $775.00 due 45 days prior to arrival
Payment payable to: The GEM Group
Email address: gerry@tourguidng.com
Payment by Visa-MasterCard or personal check- Pay Pal

Workshop dates: check www.tour-guiding.com for scheduled seminars

---

Guaranteed Results!
All of the GEM Group Workshops and Seminars are 100% SATIFISFACTION GUARANTEED Thirty Days full refund upon receipt of any GEM manual or Workshop.
Tax Credits: The Federal government offers tax credits "up to 20% of your first $5000 in expenses for tuition and other fees." This can reduce your GEM fees by as much as $195.00. These are referred to as "Lifetime Learning Credits." For more information

---

The Gem Group Since 1976

Gerald E. Mitchell, president of the GEM Group, Ltd. brings his expertise as an educator, tour operator, author, and lecturer, providing an insider's view of the travel industry. He has traveled worldwide promoting tourism in emerging countries and demonstrates a special talent for showing experienced and first-time tourists alike the beauty of the natural and cultural heritage of the destinations they visit.

Gerald's breadth of experience in developing tour programs provides a travel experience to destinations throughout the world that few can equal. He is renowned as a lecturer for both government and private industries, bringing to his audiences a depth of knowledge about the customs and indigenous populations of countries around the world that enlightens and entertains.

As an educator, Gerald Mitchell has served as adjunct professor at four U.S. universities and lectured on sustainable travel-tourism development for the Organization of American States, Canada, Russia, the Bahamas, and at the nation's military academies at West Point and Annapolis. He has served as a special advisor to the U. S. Naval Command, the U.S. Department of Commerce, and the U.S. Agency for International Development. In this last capacity, Gerald worked with the kingdom of Jordan to develop certification standards for the nation's Royal Society of Conservation, funded by Queen Noor of Jordan.

Gerald Mitchell formed the GEM Group over two decades ago to provide a quality experience for tourists to international destinations, including those in Europe, Asia, South America, Canada, and the Arctic, where he trained the Inuit tribes to conduct tours for whale watching expeditions, and along historic Native American trails. He is as much at home conducting tours in remote corners of the world as he is on the lecture podium providing training and insight into the adventure of travel for all audiences.

Mitchell is the author of a number of books on tourism and careers for those in the travel industry, including the recently published *Global Travel Tourism Career Opportunities* This is a "must read" fundamental text book for anyone considering tourism as a career. His book *Travel the World Free as an International Tour Director* has just been released in its fourth edition and provides all the fundamentals of the requirements for entering the travel industry on the international scene. Both books are now available at http://www.tour-guiding.com. Gerald Mitchell's talent and experience in the tourism industry have made him an international leader in the profession. His greatest joy over the years has been to show others the joys of travel and bring about greater understanding among the peoples of different cultures. He is truly a citizen of the world.

Made in the USA